PREACHING
WITH THE
SMALL
CONGREGATION

PREACHING
WITH THE
SMALL
CONGREGATION

Laurence A. Wagley

Abingdon Press

Nashville

Preaching with the Small Congregation

Copyright © 1989 by Abingdon Press

This book is printed on acid-free paper.

Library of Congress Cataloging-in-Publication Data

Wagley, Laurence A., 1933-
    Preaching with the small congregation / Laurence A.
Wagley.
        p.   cm.
    Bibliography: p.
    ISBN 0-687-33911-1 (alk. paper)
    1. Preaching. 2. Small churches. I. Title.
BV4221.W34   1989
251—dc20   89-31454
                                                    CIP

MANUFACTURED BY THE PARTHENON PRESS AT
NASHVILLE, TENNESSEE, UNITED STATES OF AMERICA

*To the congregations
that participate in my students' preaching*

Contents

Introduction

The Gospels report Jesus' preaching. What is surprising is how few of his sermons we have. Matthew gives us a Sermon on the Mount, but it is the author's construct and not a sermon delivered by Jesus on one occasion at a particular time.

There is much preaching by Jesus in the Gospels, but it doesn't take the form we expect—the shape we customarily call preaching.

Look at a few examples:

They came dragging a woman "taken in adultery." The Pharisees give Jesus a text from Moses. We expect Jesus to deliver a sermon on sexual morality. But what he does give is a strange sermon. He kneels and writes in the sand. There is a brief conversation with the woman, and nothing more.

On another occasion, Jesus and the disciples are preparing to leave when a young ruler comes rushing up with a question. There follows not a topical sermon on the question, but a conversation with the man. After the young ruler leaves, the disciples become involved in the issue.

There is a time when Jesus is preaching, but we get not a word of the sermon. Instead, we are told about a man let down through the roof and the exchange that takes place between Jesus, the man, and the bystanders.

Most of Jesus' sermons occur in small groups and involve dialogue with other people. Even his parables generally arise out of a question or conversation in a small group.

Jesus' preaching was participatory. It grew out of the lives of the people, used shared conversations as a common vehicle, and discovered the grace of God in social encounters.

We are beginning to congratulate ourselves that we are reclaiming the parables—Jesus' method we say. If we really want Jesus' method, we might take those narratives a step farther and discuss them with the people present. It's risky, as Jesus proved, but it's a kind of preaching that can involve small groups far more than any monologue.

There is a place to try out Jesus' dominant style of preaching. We could use it in the small congregation. We have never developed a preaching method designed just for the small membership church. Most of the literature describes the small church as hardy, but many Protestant denominations are closing small churches at an alarming rate. The United Methodist Church alone has closed 300 each year since 1967. If we developed preaching to fit the distinctive needs of the small church, more churches might stay open to experience it.

Still, there are a lot of small churches. One stands on almost every corner. Turn a curse in the country and you see a steeple. Walk down a city street and pass another small church. In a time that measures success by bigness, the small congregation has made a life-style of swimming against the current.

I grew up in such a church. If the Rhymers or Wagleys were absent, it was difficult to "have church." Later, in large urban or suburban churches, I learned that many people have nostalgia for the small congregation. Maybe that's why so many Christmas cards have small churches on them. I don't think a preference for a small congregation is a retreat into another time. Small churches are not old-fashioned or out of touch.

Small churches represent something persistent and crucial in our modern society. Sometimes multi-story office buildings and apartment complexes tower over it, but the small congregation persists as a little pocket of community amid the impersonality of the city. In spite of our admiration of bigness, the small church lodges in our hearts. Even the secular seasons of Thanksgiving, Christmas, and Easter picture a return to an intimate and caring extended family—a family around the piano singing the old songs. The old songs are hymns, and sometimes the family even pauses for prayer. That's a kind of never-never land as presented in commercials, but it is alive and well in the small membership church.

Not all small churches are loving, but they persist because we long for loving relationships. Even in this modern world, people look for their roots and try to get the family together. In spite of the urge for privacy and the hesitancy to intrude on others, there remains a deeper longing. It is a yearning for a loving family, warm and accepting, that knows our strengths and weaknesses and loves both. We yearn to belong, to be connected, to be affirmed and supported. We need a primary group that helps us remember our heritage, gives us rituals of belonging, and equips us to confront a world that remains big, alien, and cold.

The small congregation also retains the centrality of preaching and worship. This centrality is more than lack of competition from other programs. The church experience for people in the small congregation is essentially one of singing, praying, and hearing the Word.

As the small membership church fulfills needs in many peoples' lives, it also reminds and models for the big church what it means to be the Church. Without the centrality of preaching and worship and without caring relationships in primary groups, large and superficial, transcient, and fail in the only two commandments Jesus gave us.

1

Challenges to Preaching in a Small Congregation

Steve preaches twice on Sunday morning. When he and his colleagues meet on Monday, Steve talks about his sermon at the county seat church. He says Bethel, the out point, is a kind of warm-up for the sermon at First Church. Steve's frustration is that often the sermon he preaches at Bethel takes a character of its own. Instead of serving as a trial run, the sermon in the small congregation becomes a whole different kind of preaching.

Steve's preparation is the same for both sermons, but frequently Steve finds himself stepping out of the pulpit at the smaller church and moving close to the people. His carefully prepared notes get in the way, and he pushes them aside or leaves them behind. He adds stories out of the life of the little community and speaks directly to persons in the congregation. Just recently he asked a rhetorical question and was surprised to have someone from the congregation answer. Now, actual dialogue often occurs during sermons at Bethel.

The preaching Steve does at Bethel doesn't conform to models he learned at seminary. What is a preacher with such a church to do?

Many of us preachers are struggling with the distinctive

communication situation we find in small membership churches. Like Steve, we may excuse our preaching style in the small church as an aberration. We explain that our acquired style is useful only because of the unique character of the particular church we serve. No one told us that we should modify the sermon for the small congregation. Homiletical texts do not take size of congregation into consideration. Preaching courses in seminary never advise modifying the sermon for small groups.

When preachers gather, most of us talk only about our sermons to a full crowd. We excuse modification of preaching for small groups as if such change is a breach of the canons of "good preaching." Most feel that a sizable congregation is required to manage preaching and worship adequately. The impromptu modifications we make for small groups are mentioned apologetically as an example of how small churches fail to measure up to good practice.

We live in a culture that values bigness. If it is not big, loud, and expensive, it must be failing. Ministers of churches with limited attendance have been infected by the numbers virus. Rather than develop preaching that takes advantage of the particular gifts of the small membership church, we apologize for not preaching as we would to a large congregation.

Church members, too, are demoralized because they lack the size, style, and programs of the big church. They feel neglected and inferior because denominational programming tends to highlight the large church. Preaching and worship, as modeled in the literature and taught in the seminaries, emphasize raised pulpits, projection, coordination with choirs and festivals, and seem to assume large buildings and crowds of people. The small membership church feels unable to meet the standards. Ministers of these congregations remember their training and feel they have an inadequate setting for the practice of preaching. It is not surprising that members and ministers of small membership churches are demoralized and consider their practice somehow deficient. This feeling of inferiority is a self-fulfilling prophecy.

The average size for a Protestant congregation at worship in the United States is less than 75. Many larger congregations feel diminished because they remember a time when more people attended. Churches that consider themselves small represent more than a small percentage of churches in this country. They consider themselves "small" and "marginal" when "average" is a more accurate description. These congregations reflect the prevailing view that value is dependent on size.

To complicate their problems, small membership churches often conduct their preaching and worship according to models developed for other (and larger) churches. They are puzzled and frustrated when these models serve them poorly.

The essential difference between the nature of small and large churches is not generally recognized. The large church is not just an expanded version of the small church. Bigness or smallness is not a characteristic to be listed among other classifications. Size affects everything else and often changes the essential nature of the characteristic. Congregational participation is an example. As the congregation increases in size, participation generally decreases. More important, the kind of involvement practiced in the small group is simply not possible in the large congregation. The change in participation is not a matter of degree but of kind.

Preaching in the small church requires a different kind of communication than practiced when preaching in the large church. Modern preaching places emphasis on congregational participation. What has not been noted in the practice of preaching is that the *kind* of participation available to the large congregation is very different from the participation possible in the small congregation. Participation in the primary group is more intimate, and communication is colored by relationships. In the small church, the preacher may look out the window during the service and say, "John, you left your lights on." If John's lights are noticed in the large church, a note will be passed to the minister. During announcements, the minister will say, "The owner of the black 1985 Ford whose license number is W10169 has left the lights on."

In a critique published in 1967, Reuel L. Howe found conventional preaching to be deficient in four ways.

(1) Physical arrangement is poor. The pulpit is elevated, causing the preacher to look down and the people to look up. Howe noted that the elevation of the Word of God above life is a contradiction of the concept of its embodiment in the life of the people.

(2) The manner of preaching reflects the clergy's monopolistic role: the preacher speaks, and the people listen. The preacher is active. The people are passive. Preaching is usually didactic and impersonal.

(3) The content of preaching all too often demonstrates an unrelatedness of the gospel to life, which has been acquired by the preacher in an academic study of Christianity.

(4) The absence of organized response or feedback

reinforces the stereotypes people entertain about preaching.[1]

These criticisms still apply. Their remedy, however, is very different depending on the size of the church. If preaching in the small congregation is modeled after that of the large church, as is usually the case, it does feel as if the preacher is "high and lifted up" and in a monopolistic role. The sermon becomes distant, impersonal, and inauthentic.

When the Church Tries to Be What It Is Not

There are various models for worship and preaching in the small church. Unfortunately they have been designed for different kinds of churches and serve the small church poorly.

The Small Church Trying to Act Like a Big Church

This is the dominant and most available model for preaching and worship in the small membership church. You probably recognize the stereotype: A cheap electric organ has been substituted for the piano, and the people are instructed to be quiet as the organ begins the service. The people are scattered about the building, distant from one another, from the center of worship, and from the preacher. A bulletin is provided, and the order is followed without interruption. Ushers become distant and formal when they pass offering plates or when they supervise how the people receive the Lord's Supper. Exterior standards are used to judge the appropriateness of music, liturgy, and behavior. The preacher moves away from the people, ascends to a higher level, and stands behind an imposing pulpit. It is considered to be in poor taste for the preacher to make references in the sermon either to personal experiences or to situations in the lives of members of the congregation. Illustrations are generalized and usually come from a distant world. There is little emotion. It is as though the family had entered the front parlor to entertain an honored, but unfamiliar, guest. Everyone is on his or her best behavior, polite and inoffensive.

The Small Church Trying to Conduct a Perpetual Revival

Revivalistic styles of preaching are used in many small churches. These churches value the gospel, and their people remember a time when it was important to share that gospel with the many members of the community who had not experienced the faith for themselves. Some of their best memories are of revival meetings when the house was packed, worship was exciting and stimulating, and the preaching caught the attention of the whole community. Every Sunday the church tries to restage such a revival, but the conditions have changed. The sermon is preached as if the house is full of prospects for first commitment. The fact is there is no one present but loyal members. *Revival* is misnamed. It is aimed at conversion rather than renewal. The result is that today's revival sermons are addressed to people who are not in church. The sermon fails to address the people who do come. It's another case of the church trying to be what it is not.

Revival sermons also have a "bigger than life" image. Evangelistic preaching is related in the common imagination to city-wide campaigns, to television audiences, and to preachers with large followings. The local preacher responds to a mental image of a "Robert Schuller congregation" rather than preaching to the small group gathered. The preacher shouts to the imaginary large massed audience and gazes into the distance. This "bigger than life" image also encourages the congregation to become an audience—spectators who watch the performance rather than participants who join in the action. Music in the small church also lacks the big sound. Often amplifiers are added to provide a big sound even when no one has trouble hearing.

Preaching is dependent on how the sermon is heard. When the subliminal context is not provided, revival preaching loses much of its impact. It begins to feel like a charade or like a poor imitation of the real thing. Giving invitations without response can wear down both preacher and congregation. The small membership church is demoralized. There is a time for evangelistic preaching, but it is not needed as a steady diet by a small congregation made up of faithful members. In chapter 5, I will describe a preaching model that better fits the evangelistic needs of the small congregation.

The Church Reinforcing Community Moral Standards

Small congregations often want clear moral rules. There are good reasons why they want these rules reinforced. People are moving away. Young people are attracted to new and different life-styles. The very stability of the community is at risk. The church in this setting wants preaching that is dependable and that supports recognized values. Moralistic preaching is designed to remind church members of their responsibility to lead good lives, to warn them of dangers, and to call them to deeper commitment. "Ought" and "should" are common words in moralistic sermons. "Try harder" and "be more committed" become standard admonitions. Instead of grace, law is the dominant emphasis of this kind of preaching. A moralistic preacher can come from either the liberal or conservative church. The sins are different, but the prescription is the same. On one side of the aisle, the sins are personal (lying, cheating, profaning the Sabbath). On the other side of the aisle, the sins are social (racial prejudice, militarism, oppression). The preacher gives the same admonition in either case: "Stop it!"

A small membership church in the middle of a block in a changing neighborhood often likes to recall the time when "the church was full of young families." The pastor is frustrated at this "retreat into nostalgia" and at the resistance to evangelization of the people now moving into the neighborhood. The sermons tend to remind the people of their responsibility to move out in acceptance to persons of other races and national origins. One day listening to an older adult Sunday school class, the pastor realizes that the main agenda of this group is to hold on to their identity, an identity threatened by the very people their pastor is preaching to them to love.

Moralistic sermons are preached by frustrated preachers. Addressed to small, highly committed congregations, moralistic preaching produces frustrated church members. The reminders of the moralistic sermon are better fitted to the large, casual congregation that needs to move beyond superficial commitment. There is some built-in defense against such preaching in the big church where any word has less personal impact.

Moralistic styles of preaching are reinforced by an authoritarian understanding of ministry. Small churches tend to give authority to the minister. Some ministers make constructive use of this granting of power by using it to take initiative. Others become addicted to power and are threatened by anyone who seems to be taking authority they perceive as their own. The distinctive problem of an authoritarian style for the preacher is that the congregation becomes passive. Instead of entering into dialogue with the people and encouraging their participation, the authoritarian preacher "tells" them the answers. This preacher, joined by an infallible Bible and an inflexible moral code, produces a type of deductive preaching that reinforces the dominant values of the community. Not only is this a style of preaching that poorly serves the small membership church; it is also an aberration of the gospel.

The Church Trying to Be What It Used to Be

Nostalgia for the "good old days" flavors preaching and worship in some small churches like the one described above. Members remember better times when people were good and the church was full. There were more children in church then, and they were more respectful. There is a positive kind of remembering that connects people with their tradition and empowers them for the future. We will consider this kind of remembering in subsequent chapters. Nostalgia has the opposite effect, causing people to retreat into the past and robbing them of energy to face today. Constantly comparing the "good old days" to a less good present contributes to low morale. There are better alternatives.

When the Small Church Fails
to Take Advantage of What It Is

In the last ten years a significant body of material has been written for the small church, especially in the areas of education, finance, and evangelism. In the next chapter, this research is reviewed to discover the distinctive character of the small church. However, the extensive research of the small congregation has generally neglected preaching. Chapter 2 will address preaching in the small congregation and the nature of communication experienced there.

Meanwhile, we need to note that part of the problem with preaching in small congregations is that there has been little attempt to take advantage of the considerable gifts given to these churches.

The small church needs to capitalize on its smallness. Based on the root word *integer* (one, undivided number) are the words *integrity* and *integration.* Integrity means whole, complete, sound, honest. Integration is restoring wholeness. When I became the interim pastor of a small church, I discovered that a whole, undivided model of ministry has a much better chance in the small church. There are fewer distractions, and everything is integrated. Organization is simple. It's strange how the word *simple* has fallen on hard times. It is related to integrity and honesty (uncompounded, not given to duplicity). In a complex world, many people are looking for small rather than big groups. Instead of emphasizing what the church can't do because of its size, stress what small size enables. The church may not have a massed choir for Christmas, but neither can big churches gather the congregation around the piano for Christmas carols.

Intimate relationships should be affirmed in the small church. Dietrich Bonhoeffer emphasized that the group is given to us. "It is by the grace of God that a congregation is permitted to gather visibly in this world to share God's Word and sacrament." The community is God's gift to us. "The more thankfully we daily receive what is given to us, the more surely and steadily will fellowship increase and grow from day to day as God pleases."[2]

There is a rediscovery of small groups today. Intimacy doesn't result just because the group is small. The small church needs to be intentional about a special quality of friendship described best by the New Testament word *koinonia*. That group will be open to persons tired of or discarded by a technological world. At its center, however, must be a place to meet Christ, who promised to be present wherever two or three meet in his name. Sermons are personal conversations in this setting. Personal needs are named and remembered. The anniversary of a death is dealt with sensitively in the small group. The resources of Christian koinonia support the sermon and find expression in worship.

Shared experiences are central to preaching and worship in the small church. Remembering these experiences and making provision for church sharing is a strength of the small church. "Remember when . . ." stories are popular. In his book *Sunday Dinner*, Will Willimon compares The Lord's Supper to family meals.[3] He remembers the stories families tell at such meals, stories that help family members remember who they are. Such shared experiences in small, intimate groups help us all know who we are and that we are loved. It is a ministry deeply needed in this impersonal world.

Small churches are more flexible. Some people have the

opinion that small churches are rigid, opposed to change, "set in their ways." Some are. However, in small churches, fewer people have to agree to a change. Democracy is participatory democracy, like that of the town meeting. Democracy in large churches can only be representative. Decisions are made quickly in the small church to fit a specific situation. The congregation decides to hold worship at the lake, to help the family whose house burned last night, and to call everyone about praying for Martha. Wide flexibility is available for preaching and worship.

The small church can have a much more intimate level of participation in preaching than is possible in the large church. Participation in the sermon in the large church means at most a talk-back session after the sermon. More likely, participation in the large church probably means that the preacher has taken the viewpoint of members of the congregation into consideration in the preparation of the sermon. In small churches, I recommend a participatory model of preaching that includes congregational preparation and participation by the people in the actual delivery of the sermon. Today, group participation is a central methodology in education, social activities, business, and government. Group discussion is a popular television and radio format for presenting information, arriving at decisions, and telling stories. Study groups, committee meetings, and business caucuses have all turned from monologue to group participation. The small church has the option of considering congregational participation in the sermon.

The small church needs to remember its past, not with nostalgia, but as a reclaiming of its identity. Rather than trying to conform to some unrealistic model for a large suburban church, the small church needs to rediscover what has made it what it is. This is not living in the past. It is using the past as a resource for today. Retelling the stories releases their stored energy. The church is able to tap this reservoir of remembered life and free its accomplishments of the past so that it inspires new expressions.

Should we design an ideal church for our time, it would take many characteristics from the small membership church. Since many families have splintered and few people have the support the clan once provided, the ideal church would serve as an extended family. In an impersonal world, the church needs to be built on relationships, with provision for face-to-face conversation and in-depth group experience. Since large numbers of us have more complexity than we want in our jobs, let the church be a simple organization. In short, let's try to establish a church that models God's caring love for each of us and understands such loving relationships as it's reason for being.

After we have designed an ideal church for our time, we will need to design preaching to fit its distinct communication situation. Generally, we assume that a sermon prepared and delivered for 250 also fits a congregation of twenty-five, but an intimate preaching situation can differ greatly from preaching to a large church. The intimate setting needs no amplification of sound or special lighting. The pulpit doesn't need to be elevated. The preacher is much closer and can speak personally to the people present. Facial expression and body language are more obvious in the small congregation, and the preacher may use more understatement and innuendo. Local, even personal, concerns can be addressed easily and naturally. There is opportunity for congregational participation. We need more sermons whose content, shape, and style of delivery fit the distinctive needs of the small church and that take advantage of the unique opportunities offered by small groups.

A participatory sermon fits the above criteria well. Participatory preaching has received little attention because it does not fit the communication situation of the large church. It does hone skills that will be useful in preaching to the large group. However, its primary design is for the small group, where the whole community of God can grow by active and vocal participation in the sermon.

The particular needs of the small membership church are beginning to call new models for preaching into being.

One Sunday at Bethel things really got out of hand. During the raising of concerns for prayer, Barbara asked for prayers for her mother. Nancy inquired, "How is your mother doing, Barbara?" Barbara's answer was to burst into tears.

The little congregation didn't lapse into embarrassed silence and back away. John took Barbara's hand and said, "I know your mother's having a hard time."

Barbara's response was sharp. "Yes, and the rest of us are having a hard time too!" That brought on more tears. Steve had the sense to wait and not interrupt or move on to other concerns.

Barbara was now whispering softly, "I'm sorry. . . . I'm sorry."

Everyone in the church knew that Barbara had moved her mother into her own home two years ago. They also knew what a strain the constant care of her mother had been for both Barbara and the rest of her family. Barbara once was vivacious and outgoing. She had been superintendent of the Sunday school and involved in almost everything the church did. Now, she often missed church and appeared in town only to pick up groceries.

Barbara dried her eyes. "You all know I love my mother. It's just that sometimes I don't have any living left for myself. Bob helps every way he can, but sometimes he loses patience, and the kids are growing up without me. I do want your prayers for Mother, but I also want your prayers for me and the rest of the family. Recently we've been talking about putting Mother in Elms Nursing Home."

Steve never preached the sermon he had prepared that Sunday. Driving away from the church, he reflected that the rest of the service felt more like a group counseling session than a worship service. He knew that his ability to listen and ask the right questions had helped. He had been surprised when Tom quoted the scripture passage Steve had just read, and members of the congregation used it to talk to Barbara about God's love and concern for her and her family.

What had begun in the raising of concerns for prayer had moved into sharing of stories, conversation about options, and finally into a prayer period that reflected the love and concern both of the members of the congregation and of God. In spite of himself, Steve couldn't regret that his prepared sermon had never been delivered. He suspected that more of the gospel had been proclaimed and heard that Sunday morning than in most services.

Experiences like Barbara's request for prayer caused Steve to begin reassessing the kind of preaching that best served his small membership church. He was beginning to recognize that a different kind of communication situation existed at Bethel than at the larger county seat church.

C H A P T E R

2

Communication in the Small Congregation

When the small membership church meets for worship and preaching, it is a distinctive community and is quite different from its big neighboring church. Face-to-face relationships encourage intimacy, and in many settings this intimacy encourages relationships that support community.

People look around the group and call one another by name. They have shared many experiences during the week, and now they review those experiences and "catch each other up." The sanctuary is an extension of the people's homes. Members take pride in the building. They clean and repair it themselves. The people are friends and family. Each person makes what contribution he or she can to the common worship of the group. People know one another, and their sharing may have the abrasiveness or affection of family life. Personal and community concerns are discussed and dealt with. There is sincere inquiry about people who are sick, out of work, or have other problems. They believe that the way they see things is the way they really are. There is an ongoing struggle to provide stability in the community. Conflict is highly personal, and divisions split families and friends. People value continuity and are suspicious of change.

What happens in this setting? Relationships are

reinforced. Members are told and shown that they are loved. People touch. Experiences are remembered, and plans are made for the future. It is all right to interrupt worship to deal with personal needs. There is room for laughter, anger, grief, and anticipation. God is experienced as being personal and caring. Breaks in communication are the kind that occur in families. Exclusion is a powerful threat.

The preacher is one of the family. The sermon is the high point of the morning. It includes personal anecdotes and community happenings. The preacher is a personal friend, quite aside from his or her ability to preach or to be competent in the skills of ministry. The sermon is conversational, and members feel they are participating in a dialogue even if they don't say a word. It is all right for the preacher to address members of the congregation by name and for them to respond.

Not every small membership church incorporates all these traits, but they do frequently occur whether the church is rural or urban. They are characteristics of size and not of region, nationality, culture, or density of population.

There is a great deal of research and writing about the small membership church. Much of this attention is sociological. This research points out that most Protestant churches are small, with the average having fewer than seventy-five people in Sunday morning worship. One fourth have fewer than thirty-five.[1]

The unique character of the small church may be summarized as follows.

+ High priority on relationships[2]
+ Importance of the primary group[3]

+ More shared experiences[4]
+ High participation in worship[5]
+ High participation in management of the church[6]
+ Primacy of lay leadership[7]
+ Informal communications system[8]
+ Importance of family relationships[9]
+ Simple organization[10]
+ Intergenerational organization[11]
+ Importance of passages in the family—births, baptisms, weddings, deaths[12]
+ Tendency to maintain size, outlook, and ways of doing things[13]

These general characteristics are confirmed by the sociological research of several authors,[14] and has been appropriated by areas of study—particularly education, finance and church administration, and evangelism.[15]

The Uniqueness of the Communication Situation

"The preacher" is the name for clergy in most small churches. It is more than a title. "The preacher" names the clergy after the most prominent activity in which the laity see the pastor involved. Surveys that name and rate the areas of ministry customarily put preaching at the top of the list. Many small churches ask little more of their clergy than a good sermon on Sunday. There are several reasons why. Their preachers often work at other jobs. Lacking secular jobs, they probably serve multiple churches. A perennial joke in small churches is that the preacher is paid for just one hour of work a week. It is in good humor and is not intended as either a reflection on the amount of work done or the amount of money paid. It is not neglect of other duties that causes clergy to be called "the preacher." Preaching is the central event of the church week. It is the time most members of the church gather, and in the small church a greater percentage of the members attend the Sunday service than in larger churches. People in small congregations gather for what is persistently called, "the preaching service."

"The preaching service" includes singing, praying, scripture lessons, forms of sharing, and sometimes the sacraments, but the centerpiece is the sermon.

The sermon comes as the climax of most small church services. Often other parts of the service are neglected, but the sermon is never omitted.

Part of the reason for the centrality of preaching in the small church is the uniqueness of the communication situation. When clergy are called "the preacher" and worship is referred to as "the preaching service," it is apparent that a distinctive communication situation has come into being.

Several studies mention the importance of preaching and worship in the small church. Preaching, however, is generally noted in relationship to the primary subject under consideration (education, administration, evangelism, and so on). There has been little treatment of the special communication situation found in the small church. Implications for preaching of the special nature of the small congregation have been ignored.

The unique communication situation endemic to the small congregation has three aspects:

Community. The church with small attendance is characterized by closeness, by shared concerns, by knowledge and understanding of one another, and by relation. Closeness is first a matter of space. The effect of physical closeness is generally that people speak softly, but also with a tendency toward honesty and directness. The preacher and the congregation are literally face-to-face. It's easy to see facial expression and body language. Hearing is more acute. Communication is more intelligible. Closeness also describes relationship. Communication in this setting is the kind that occurs in primary groups or when "family matters" are discussed. The word *relation* refers to both an act of relating (telling) and family relationship. It is a family-like setting. Sometimes literally two or three families make up the congregation. People who are not kin still are part of the extended family, and they share family values, concerns, and secrets. In this situation, an intimate and direct communication style is natural.

The communication situation in the small church also is marked by shared experiences. The congregation doesn't have to be "brought on board" or initiated. However, an outsider is sometimes "lost" and doesn't know what is being said. Members of the group have moved rapidly past perfunctory and introductory concerns. At its optimum, the communication situation is connected with the life of the community. In most small churches, the members of the congregation live in a neighborhood where they are in daily contact with one another. Even in large cities, members of a small congregation will often stay in touch. Pastoral day-to-day meetings with members of the congregation keep the minister in touch with the people. Issues having to do with daily concerns are more likely to be included in church discussions than where such regular contact is lacking. If the preacher lives among the people in the small community, there is opportunity to know the preacher well. A relationship of trust can grow and mature among members of the congregation and between congregation and preacher. This is contrasted with large churches, which "lack pastoral, day-to-day encounters with the total life of God's people which is a prerequisite for faithfulness to the word."[16]

Members of the community know one another and have a sense of being known. Sincerity, insight, and understanding are emphasized in this setting.

The communication situation is also influenced by a freedom to act and speak that generally characterizes the small church. Such freedom exercised in social and administrative settings tends to generate more of a sense of freedom and extends to worship and preaching. This social interaction is informal and is a speech system that is unique to this setting. Some groups have their own accent or language, which is given a special hearing when members speak. This is recognized in, but not limited to, ethnic groups.

Conflict is more personality than issue-oriented. Disagreement is feared because it has the potential of splitting families and dividing the community. Some small communities have observed the boundaries of such divisions for decades.

Sharing. Small churches share stories. Stories work best in primary groups where people know one another. Members have a common identity partly because they can spin a common thread through all their lives. Stories arise out of the stuff of shared experience and shared tradition.

Common tradition creates a distinctive communication situation. Whether it's family history, sense of place, or common church relationship, tradition takes an important role in the small church. Tradition helps a person or a community know who they are. Values pass from one

generation to the next. The continuity between generations enables inter-generational relationships. Each new
generation is given a sense of being connected to the
community and gains a sense of belonging.

Stories and rituals are effective means of passing and
maintaining traditions. Oral tradition thrives in small
groups where stories can be repeated with regularity. The
environment is dependable. This has the effect of helping
children know what is possible, and it develops a balance
between an environment that is too open or too closed.
Characterization is developed, so children know what
kind of people their forbears are. Plot is based on meaning
and purpose, so the sequence of happenings in people's
lives has significance. Storytellers not only enable
members of the community to remember, but also they
help people relive the history of the group.

A child comes running to Mother, kisses her, and hands
her a wildflower picked from the field. That moment may
be relived for generations as the pressed flower is
displayed and the story retold. The construction of the
church building, hanging of paintings, and personal
experiences and happenings in the church are retold and
are given a contemporary life.

Stories have the greatest impact when hearers identify
with both the storyteller and the story itself. Sharing of
stories is a multi-dimensional process that includes the
skill of the storyteller, the trust placed in the story and the
teller, and the environment provided by the group. This
dynamic interaction is formative of individual members
and of the group itself.

The central story of the church, the gospel, is shared in a
similar way. As trusted storytellers share the gospel, it has
contemporary meaning for members of the small group.

The community revisits the events of Jesus' life. As the story is told, members of the group see themselves in the crowds around Jesus. They experience the joy and grief. Then as they come to see the story of the gospel through the lens of Jesus' death and resurrection, a new way of understanding their own life and death is provided. This becomes a pattern in which God's act in Jesus Christ is seen by the community as a paradigm. The community and individual lives are given meaning as they conform to this model. This world view shapes the communication situation of the group that shares it.

Participation. The communication situation in the small church is molded by the expectation of participation. In a group of two hundred or more, participation must be severely limited. In the small congregation, most members have some active role in the administration of the church and in conducting the worship service.

Vocal participation is also possible in the small church. The lack of opportunity for vocal participation in the large church serves as a brake on other forms of response. There is a symbiotic relationship between vocal participation and a feeling of investment. In discussion, people can test ideas and see whether they apply to personal problems. In the small church, the group is small enough for people to respond, to say yes. Conversation is possible—real conversation. Members contribute as well as receive and have a deeper feeling of investment. It is easy to become uninvolved in one-way communication. Dialogue and group discussion have a much deeper level of participation and investment by members of the group.

Participation is possible in follow-up. People feel that their participation "makes a difference." Final decisions and actions will be determined by church members. This level of sharing of responsibility makes a real difference in the communication situation that exists in the small church.

Recognizing and Improving the Communication Situation

The communication situation in the small church that calls for community, sharing, and participation is often frustrated. In chapter 1, we looked at several models of preaching that fail because they are designed for a communication situation other than that of the small congregation. There are ways of recognizing and improving the communication situation in the small membership church.

Create an Environment for Sharing

The building is almost always designed for preaching. The pulpit occupies the focal point of the sanctuary. The pews are gathered facing the pulpit as the seats in a theater face the stage.

However, in most cases the congregation has ceased to use the building in the way it was planned. The congregation, unlike the building, is really community centered, and the community gathers in the back of the church near the entrance. Sometimes this is under a balcony. In any case, this gathering place leaves the preacher isolated in the other end of the sanctuary. Music, particularly congregational singing, is frustrated in this arrangement. The piano is also isolated, and the pianist's back is to the congregation. Some members of the congregation will move toward the preacher, which has the effect of scattering the people. Gathered prayer and the sacraments are even more handicapped because there is little space for either and movement is difficult. Reading of scripture and other spoken words are hard to hear. A public address system is often added, even in very small buildings. It seldom takes acoustics into consideration and sounds hollow, impersonal, and phony.

The pulpit, designed to stand as a tribute to preaching, literally forces people near the front to look up to the preacher. The preacher may try to shout across the empty pews to the little congregation near the rear of the building. In fact, a strained, loud, and singsong vocal quality is often identified with preaching.

When preaching is defined in terms of community, the environment can often be modified to better fit the communication situation. If there is a choir, it should sing in the midst of the congregation rather than isolated and on display in a choir loft. The preacher can also move toward the congregation and adopt a stance and manner that communicates that the sermon is a sharing between friends. The congregation should find a way to gather than encourages a feeling of relatedness and closeness.

The environment should allow the people to gather as in one of their homes. The style of gathering will vary as to whether the meal is to be held in the dining room or at the kitchen table, but in any case, the gathering should be on a family scale.

My home church had two major liturgical centers: the pulpit and the potbellied stove. The stove was much like the one at the neighborhood store, where people gathered to converse and to swap stories before they bought their groceries. Around the stove at church there is a similar exchange. It is an important preparation for worship. An occasional seminary student will attempt to shorten this period of visitation in the small church and exhort the people, "If you must talk, talk quietly to God." That student has not understood the close connection in the small church between relationship with the folks and relationship with God. Relationship is expressed in many ways in the worship of the small congregation—singing together, gathering for prayer, sharing concerns, passing the peace, and so on.

In small churches, the communication situation is influenced by the Sunday school class. Many churches have depended on the Sunday school for their basic Sunday observance. Often the Sunday school meets every week, but the worship service is held on a less frequent basis. Some churches have survived for long periods with no worship service at all. The class has often been shaped to fit the distinctive needs of the small church. Occasionally the teacher has continued lecturing—a behavior modeled after the sermon. More often, there is a shared leadership, or at least a discussion format where members of the class are expected to participate.

Though gathering into discussion groups seems to come naturally to the small congregation, there can be resistance if someone tries to force it. If you want to gather the people into a more contiguous group, as I often want to with a participatory model of preaching, you need to know the congregation. Persons may let their wish to be cooperative rule over their regard for their own place. Others refuse to move or grumble about the intrusion on their space. Powerful forces are at work here, having to do with the way the congregation sees itself. When a person sits in a particular pew in the small church, that person knows who will be sitting on the left and the right and who is ahead and behind. The whole worship experience is taken in from that particular perspective. If someone is absent or not in the accustomed place, the worship experience is altered. There is even memory of where family members who have died use to sit, and their memories are still honored. Take some care with changing the seating arrangement. A small church is closely identified with its house of worship and with the furniture inside. Congregations often experience a period of unease when they move to a new building or when new furnishings are provided for the church.

How, then, is it possible to gather the congregation on those occasions when a contiguous seating pattern is needed? Help them see, worship and preaching from a different perspective. If most people understand the purpose, share in the intention, and see the new picture, they will move willingly. Announcements in advance of a participatory sermon will prepare the people to be seated close together. As a congregation uses its building for participation, they may decide to alter the floor plan and furnishings. If there is more seating than needed, extra pews may be moved into conversational groupings as a gathering place before and after worship. As the people have a changed image of themselves, they can sit in different places or even change the places.

Involve the Congregation in Preparation

Preaching in the small church would be dramatically improved if the people were involved in its preparation. Why is the sermon the minister's secret? When the people participate in every other aspect of community life, why can't they share in the preparation of the sermon? Instead, preachers act as though the sermon were a secret imparted to them alone to be unveiled on Sunday morning.

In the small church, worship is holistic. The worship itself is the primary occasion for everything the church does—education, missions, evangelism, raising money, cultural and artistic emphasis, and even social activities. Not much is relegated to other times and places or given to committees to work out. If the people were allowed to aid in preparation, both preaching and worship would be integrated into all other concerns of the community.

Preparation by the church should be quality preparation, not busy work. Let the people know what the text is. Encourage them to study it with care. Why is Bible study so often isolated from other church activities, including the sermon? Include the people in preparation for worship. What worship activities would support the sermon? What kind of music would help? It's strange that in churches of all sizes no provision is made for this kind of preparation.

The study group was working its way through the fourth chapter of Luke, where there is mention of Jesus' healing of Peter's mother-in-law. Alice interrupted, "Preacher, I forgot to tell you that Henrietta is really sick."

"Why did you think of Henrietta just now?"

"Well, I guess because we were talking about sickness and healing—and because Henrietta is a lot like Peter's mother-in-law. Her family needs for her to get up and serve the meals! It's like the whole family is laid up when Henrietta is sick."

Regular preparation develops a network of resources. People with special skills, knowledge, and experiences can be on call. Small churches underestimate their resources and neglect the talents of their people. Who can tell a story well? Is there someone who can provide photography? Is there a student who will visit a library and make a report? Who keeps abreast of special interests, such as markets, art, and stamps? Are there people who keep informed about the news? There must be members who keep in touch with shut-ins or persons who have moved away.

A church should begin a library and learn to use it. Some libraries are unused because the church provides no occasions for its use. Participatory preaching will send people to the books.

Preparation for preaching is good Christian education. Novices indulge in strange arguments about biblical interpretation. Mature students who have had opportunity to study the issues and to be involved in shaping church interpretation learn to disagree and still be family. Instead of fearing disagreement, a study group begins to experience disagreement as an occasion for growth. Bible study becomes preparation for both preaching and life.

Worship and preaching can be a catching up of the whole week and a celebration of it. The experiences of the community take story form and become permanent resources for preaching.

Establish Participation in the Whole Service

Involvement of the laity is popular among large churches now. Someone reads the scripture lessons and so they have met their goal. Participation is much more important and organic in the small church. "Individuals in a worshiping body of fifty know that their presence and absence are noticed, that their voices make a difference in the singing and speaking, that their body language is read, that their money in the offering is important, and that a large percentage have a specific responsibility."[17]

Participatory worship helps people do what they do best. It is not a self conscious parading of laity. Sometimes we turn to wrong solutions for lay involvement in worship. Don't post a sign-up list for people to read the scripture; find the people who read it with most impact.

The single most important improvement in the worship of most churches would be the improvement of congregational singing. In large churches, congregational singing seems second rate to the professionalism of the choirs. Don't let the architecture, the organist, or the choir take congregational singing away from the people. Without choirs, or even good accompaniment, small churches often have excellent congregational singing.

Prayers, sharing, passing the peace, the Lord's Supper—these are expressions of meaningful participation. There is action, participation, and interchange. Another advantage of the small congregation is its ability to move. Many churches have architecturally bound their congregations. Small congregations, however, can find their way around most of the barriers we set up.

Small churches also encourage all their members to offer their abilities to God. Some of these gifts are inappropriate, and some are poorly done, but members of the small congregation welcome the second-grade piano solo. They are concerned about enabling the gift of the person rather than judging it.

Repetition takes a different role in the small church. In the large church very little is repeated; in the small church everything is. "Sing them over again to me, wonderful words of life"—The hymn reports what happens: fondly remembered stories repeated again and again, songs we love sung over and over, special music requested, testimonies told and prayers prayed often enough so everyone knows the words. There are "in jokes," and someone saying, "Do you remember when. . . ."

Establishing an active participation in the worship service prepares the congregation for taking part during the sermon. In most settings, sermon time is very quiet participation. Other congregations still speak in a kind of ecstatic punctuation to the words of the preacher. Some speak with body language, but dialogue is maintained. I will provide a more active means of participation in the models that follow.

Relate Acts of Worship to Preaching

In the communication situation of the small church, preaching should not be considered in isolation. The people and their worship need to be closely associated with the sermon.

The scriptural base of the sermon should be evident. It is not enough for the preacher to read a few verses. A systematic approach to the study of the Bible is needed. The whole congregation is encouraged to study the lessons. A bible study group can help in preparation. The lessons should be well read. A brief introduction, good oral communication, and occasional participation by the congregation are helpful. Some churches use pew Bibles or printed lessons in the bulletin. With printed lessons, the congregation can follow the reading carefully. I prefer that the oral quality of narrative be emphasized. If the people have read the lesson in advance, their attention can be focused, and they can have deep involvement in the act of reading. Often the congregation will retell the biblical story as part of the sermon.

Prayer is less frequently related to the sermon than the reading of the lessons, but it is more likely to reveal the minister's pastoral concern for the people. Such a concern is central to preaching. If the congregation has participated in gathering prayer concerns, members are ready to pray together and to discuss their prayer concerns in the sermon. The preacher's sensitivity will be valued by the small church.

Provision for response to the sermon is provided by some orders of worship. Many small congregations have become accustomed to this form of participation in preaching. The sermon is not complete until the preacher has called for some response from the people.

The sacraments are a particular response to the sermon. The congregation is asked to move, to come forward, and to participate in the sacrament. The Lord's Supper can have a particular level of intimacy in the small church. Prayer by the gathered congregation can have a sacramental quality.

Emphasize Narrative

The sharing of stories is central to the small church and is the primal scriptural vehicle. Conventional preaching sacrificed storytelling in favor of conceptual speech flavored with "illustrations." Recently the field of homiletics has seen a return to the use of narrative in preaching. There are many good reasons for the resurgence of story. An extensive literature is now provided for this kind of preaching.[18]

The small church, however, is the best setting for

storytelling. Storytelling is a participatory art. People need a feeling of investment in the story if the telling is to have impact. Therefore, the rich narrative lode of the Bible should be mined for use in the small congregation.

A Theology of the Word for the Small Church

A church based on relationships must not forget that its primary relationship is to Jesus Christ. Otherwise the church is no different from clubs and social institutions. The small church enjoys close face-to-face relationships. It may be the hub around which the community revolves. It may be the organizing principle for the lives of many members. It provides educational, ethical, charitable, and social activities. Its identity, however, is given to the church by none of these things. The identity of the small church must be solely in its relationship to Jesus Christ. This has significant implications for the church's life and witness.

The small church is family, but it is not just the kin meeting in this place. It is the local expression of the universal family of God. The small congregation especially needs to be intentional about providing for expressions of its catholicity and universality. The minister is an important expression of connection with synod, presbytery, or conference. The minister should also be a reminder of connectedness to the whole family of God. Modern communication and transportation have done much to break down isolation. Parochialism betrays narrowness in theology as well as in world view.

The church is a redemptive society. Whatever ails the people is likely to be the business of the small church. Saving people, forgiving sins, healing mind and body, and mending relationships are activities that have been fenced into a narrow slice of life and limited to local and personal concerns. This limitation forgets how our personal needs reach around the world today. Such limitation forgets the nature of the gospel. In the redemptive church of Jesus Christ, the agony of the world becomes ours. The liberation of the oppressed everywhere becomes our mission. Reconciliation of the estranged and pacification of the warring must become part of the redemptive work of the small church.

"Small" is not a value judgment or a limitation of the mission of the church. The "small" church does not have a partial gospel because of its size. Such a church has all the resources of God.

The centrality of preaching in the small church is supported by a strong doctrine of the Word. It remembers that Jesus' preaching and Jesus' person cannot be separated. Jesus' Word is central to his whole mission. His word proclaims the nearness of God and the salvation of humanity. Jesus incarnates this message and in his death and resurrection brings it about. The early church accepted Jesus' Word as its reason for being and proclaimed its experience of the new reality Jesus had made possible.

There is a word in preaching that is formative of the lives and words of the congregation. I see this as an intimate word. It is the caring word that passes between people who love each other. It is a word that forms and cements community. Most of us remember times when such words were spoken to us person to person or in a small group. We understand ourselves because we have been addressed in such a way. Much of our self-identity comes from the context in which we were raised. From that context we learn our values and have communicated to us our sense of personal worth.

The word of preaching is also formative of new words in the receiver's mind. Where there were broken sentences and partial self-understanding, this preached word comes and helps us put into words what could not be named before. Now, with the help of this new word, we can communicate with others. Witnessing is part of the faith. The communal speaking of faith has been part of preaching from the beginning. Such sharing should be part of preaching in the modern church. It is welcomed in the small church.

Jesus, as preacher, was not a heroic presence. His emphasis on the suffering servant passages in Isaiah causes us to picture him as weak, vulnerable, and unattractive. "A poor man as liberator of the poor, a vulnerable man as savior of the helpless—that seems like a contradiction in terms."[19]

In a similar way the small church and its pastor may incarnate Jesus' message. Preaching the Word to small groups without ostentation is a way of keeping faith with a Christ who "out of his poverty brought riches to many" (II Cor. 8:9).

Such preaching of the Word might look like the following preaching event.

Preacher: The sermon for this morning is based on our reading of Matthew 11:2-6. It reminds us of the distinctive nature of Jesus' mission. We take this passage as an invitation to explore the unique nature of our church and our mission. Again today, we will talk together. That kind of preaching fits who we are and works well in our church.

Reader: "Now when John heard in prison about the deeds of the Christ, he sent word by his disciples and said to him, 'Are you he who is to come, or shall we look for another?' And Jesus answered them, 'Go and tell John what you hear and see: the blind receive their sight and the lame walk, lepers are cleansed and the deaf hear, and the dead are raised up, and the poor have good news preached to them. And blessed is he who takes no offense at me'" (Matt. 11:2-6 RSV).

Preacher: John's disciples came to Jesus and asked, "Are you the one we've been expecting, or do we look elsewhere?" What were they asking?

Response: They wanted to know if Jesus was the Messiah, if he was the one to bring the promised reign of God.

Preacher: We are gathered here this morning as Jesus' disciples. Do you think anyone is asking us a similar question?

Response: Every time a new person comes to church, he or she is asking that question.

Preacher: What do you mean?

Response: People hear great claims about the church. They come to see if our church lives up to its name.

Preacher: You think they're coming to see if this group of disciples embodies what the church should be? Karl Barth said that when people come to church they are asking, "Is it true?"

Response: Yes, I think that's right. They are asking, "Are the church's claims true for me?"

Preacher: Let's assume that a representative group from this community came to our church. They ask, "Are you the true church of Jesus Christ, or do we look for another church?" How do you respond?

Response: We try to be a true church.

Response: We don't claim we're the only church, but we try to be a faithful church.

Preacher: What will be convincing to outsiders that we are a true group of disciples?

Response: Well, they would know about our thrift shop, which provides clothes for poor people, and our meals-on-wheels for shut-ins. Those are ways of showing we are the church.

Response: I'd ask them to come and get acquainted to see how friendly and caring we are.

Response: When anyone is having problems, Reva bakes brownies and takes them by.

Response: I do that because when Sam died you all were family to me.

Preacher: Does that sound like Jesus' answer to John's disciples?

Response: He said the blind are able to see; the lame walk; lepers are healed; people are raised from the dead; and the poor have the good news preached to them.

Response: We give money to support hospitals, but I think it might be more convincing to people looking for a church to know that we care for one another.

Response: When I was laid up last fall, Joe and Ralph got my crops out of the field. That's sure helping the lame walk.

Preacher: Are there other things we could do to be the church of Jesus Christ in this community?

Response: I'd invite visitors to stay for church. I don't know if they're poor or not, but it couldn't hurt them to hear the gospel preached!

Response: I don't know about things we could do, but I do know that when I'm here I feel that this is the church of Jesus Christ.

Preacher: Then it's not so much what we do. It's what we are?

Response: Exactly! Often there's nothing to be done, but the church people can be there with us. It's not anything you do; it's just that I know you're there.

In a world where the sermon is central and the communication situation unique, special attention should be given to providing models for preaching that reflect the small church environment. In chapter 3 we turn to such models.

3

Opening the Door to Participatory Preaching

Participatory preaching often grows out of pastoral care.

The pastor stops by the little house where the shades are drawn. She waits for the shuffling answer to the door bell. They sit in the dark room, the pastor listens to the complaint of the old woman's rocker, and finally speaks.

"It's been about a year and a half now, hasn't it?"

The woman leans forward and responds immediately. "Two years the twentieth of next month."

"How are you doing?"

"About the same. We lived together for fifty-five years, and we had our good times and bad, but. . . ." The word hangs in the air. She finally sighs and abandons the thought.

"Mary, have you read the epistle lesson for Sunday?"

"First Corinthians 15? Yes."

"Is there anything in that chapter for you?"

"Yes, but I keep coming back to, 'The last enemy to be defeated will be death.' A chapter full of promises, and I hear only the problem."

"That's a place to begin. Could we talk about that as the beginning of the sermon Sunday?"

"Like you did with Emily last week?"

"Yes."

"I suppose so."

Sunday, everyone comes prepared to talk about Paul's words on the resurrection, but the sermon begins with a quiet conversation between the preacher and Mary about how hard it is to come to terms with death.

As Mary talks, the little congregation leans closer. Someone takes Mary's hand.

The sermon begins with tears and quiet nods as Mary talks publicly for the first time about a grief they all understand.

There are many ways to open the door to participatory preaching. Some of the ways have to do with congregational understanding of the nature of preaching. In churches where the preacher-congregation communication has been personal and conversational, participatory preaching can be introduced with little difficulty.

A church school class may have set the style. All that is needed is clear directions and a methodology that prepares the people to participate. Other churches may require more careful preparation that includes both a new understanding of what preaching is intended to be and a gradual introduction to the skills required in participatory preaching.

God's Word is always personal, but sermons often don't seem very intimate. There are internal and external distractions. Still, we all remember times when it seemed that the preacher was speaking "just to me." At those times the sermon comes closest to being a word from God. God's Word is God taking the initiative and coming to us. It is presence as well as communication. It comes at several levels at the same time. It is self-validating. This personal word from God changes our perspective and our situation. Our response is part of the event of the Word—God's initiative and our response seem to be connected, each a part of the whole. "Hearing" and "knowing" in Hebrew refer to a personal relationship with God.

The optimum setting for this kind of speaking and hearing is the small group. As groups grow larger they become more impersonal. In larger groups the speaker is distant, and there are more distractions. In an extended family, there is a sensed communal support, a sharing of personal feelings so that it is safe to hear intimate address and to respond with our whole being. Personal words in this kind of environment can evoke deep inner feelings and help us deal with these feelings. This is the reason group therapy is effective. Such personal address is also persuasion. We know the speaker understands and has taken our own situation into consideration.

Imaging of the church in the New Testament is one of personal care between members. If one suffers, all suffer. If one is honored, all rejoice (see I Cor. 12:25). Relationships between members of the New Testament church grow directly out of the prior relationship with God. Loving relationship is incarnated in Jesus Christ. Jesus assures the church, "As the Father has loved me, so have I loved you" (John 15:9). In fact, the church is constituted by the presence of Jesus Christ. In Revelation, this is a grand presence (see Rev. 7:15). Elsewhere the presence of Jesus Christ to the church is intimate and caring (see Matt. 18:20; I Pet. 5:7). It is a reminder of the familial relationship Hosea describes (chap. 11) and of the close, protective relationship between Yahweh and

Moses. Exodus 33 reports a personal conversation between God and Moses about how Moses is to be a credible communicator for God to the people. Moses requests God's presence. God says to Moses, "This very thing that you have spoken I will do; for you have found favor in my sight, and I know you by name" (Exod. 33:17). As a demonstration of God's presence, Moses is placed by God in "a cleft of the rock," and Moses is shielded by the hand of God so that the glory of God may not strike him dead. It is in that intimate relationship that the Tablet of the Law is given.

In the intimate setting of the small church, pastoral care can be an intentional part of the preaching of the Law and the gospel. The roles of preacher and pastoral counselor are not separated. Pastoral contacts during the week deeply influence the sermon. The preacher listens in order to speak on Sunday. Members of the intimate community hear the sermon with special sensitivity. They hear between the lines, sense pastoral intention, and receive relational as well as discursive messages. "When the preacher and the parishioners give themselves fully to the content and dynamics of the sermon, all are vulnerable, speaker and listener, to each other."[1] In such an intimate setting, it's not unusual for the preacher to notice an unexpected response during a sermon—a response that is understood because of the pastoral care context.

The setting of the small church is also the fairest environment in which to deal with prophetic issues. Prophetic and controversial issues become impersonal in large groups. Members cannot demand equal time; they go away unheard and angry. There is a sense of impotence. "There's nothing I can do about it!" In the intimate setting, prophetic issues are heard as personal words. Local and immediate issues must be taken into consideration. There is opportunity to correct the speaker and to voice another viewpoint or interpretation. There is also opportunity to take immediate action to support the prophetic witness. The small church is often not good at long-range planning, but it is good at responding to immediate needs. The small church will welcome an opportunity to discuss issues, make decisions, and take immediate action. A sermon emphasizing the personal Word of God is given an immediate hearing and often results in direct action.

Because of the personal nature of communication in the small church and the rich interplay of responses, distinctive styles of preaching are possible. These are participatory styles. I will begin with a preaching method in which only the preacher speaks, but that emphasizes dialogue between preacher and people. Then I will describe a method in which the preacher begins and the people respond. Finally, I will move to models that provide full congregational participation.

Dialogic Preaching

I have noted in chapter 1 how Reuel Howe effectively diagnoses the problems of conventional preaching as a lack of dialogue. He also supplies a model for dialogic preaching that corrects many of the deficiencies he names. He broadens the communication that takes place in preaching and develops the "partnership" that must be established between preacher and listener.

Preaching is more than transmitting ideas. "Preaching is an encounter involving not only content but relationship, not only ideas but action, not only logic but emotion, not only understanding but commitment."[2] The listeners are taken into relationship in this kind of preaching, and a "transactional process" is established.

Howe says laypeople should be involved:

(1) Because they are a part of the church. They are not intended to be passive recipients, but active participants in the witness of the church in the world.

(2) Because the experiences and insights of the people must be taken into consideration if worship is to represent a true meeting between the people and God.

(3) Because God speaks through all the people.

Howe defines dialogue as "that address and response between persons in which there is a flow of meaning between them in spite of all the obstacles that normally would block the relationship."[3] Each person presents himself or herself honestly without unfairly trying to impose his or her own views on the other.

The reader would expect from Howe's opening chapters that he would move on to a method of preaching that involves actual dialogue, active give-and-take between participants as in normal conversation. Howe often describes his method in these terms, but he avoids including the congregation in audible communication by distinguishing between the *method* of dialogue and the *principle* of dialogue. By method, he means the whole concern that governs the communication:

When the monological principle is employed, one person tells another what he ought to know, and the communication is content-centered; when the dialogical principle governs a communication, the speaker feels responsible for and responds to the patterns of experience and understanding that [the] listener brings to the situation, and thus the listener is encouraged to grapple with his own meaning in relation to the speaker's meaning.

When we make this distinction between method and principle, we can readily see that a communication which in terms of method is monologue [one speaker] may at the same time be governed by the principle of dialogue.[4]

In chapter 7 of his book, Howe gives an illustration. Students in his seminar attend a service in which the preacher delivers a sermon on I Corinthians 13 and states that love is the greatest power in the world. Following the service a group discusses the sermon in the preacher's absence. In that discussion, a president of a small company takes sharp exception to the sermon, saying that methods the preacher advocated would not work in a highly competitive field. However, as the president describes the difficulties of practicing love in his business, another member of the group asks him how he survives. "I would say that I am helped by remembering that my associates, competitors, and customers are persons; that I should respect them and treat them as persons." Howe responds, "Although earlier in commenting on the sermon he had said that the practice of Christian love was impractical, he now in his own terms rather than in the theological terms of the preacher was witnessing to the power of personal regard in his business life."[5]

I am puzzled why Howe does not use a dialogic style in both method and principle. His illustration is of a group in active conversation—following the sermon. I think they might have come to such insight had dialogue been used during the sermon itself. However, since Howe's work was an early breakthrough in the application of principles of dialogue to preaching, I recommend it before I move on to models that are dialogic in both method and principle. I also think it is an excellent way to open the door to participatory preaching.

Howe emphasizes preaching as a cooperative activity. The preacher should find ways to draw upon the resources of the people. He recommends study groups as an arena where the preacher can learn the relevance of scripture passages to the lives of the people. His intention is to stand in the pulpit and speak for, instead of to, the people.

Howe's definition of the preacher's role as one of dialogue and his emphasis on the responsibility of the laity for preaching lay the groundwork for fuller participation. His work makes a significant contribution to altering the perceived communication situation in which the preacher is supposed to speak and the people listen. His emphasis on finding ways to promote dialogue before and after preaching is a helpful way of getting a congregation ready for participatory preaching.

Howe's approach to preaching also identifies the preacher as a member of the community. This is particularly important in a small church where the preacher needs to be known as a whole person, whose life as well as witness support the gospel. Such a preacher understands the spoken and unspoken values of the community, can speak to the concerns and in the accents of the people, and is approachable and helpful in the several arenas of ministry.

Feedback to the Sermon

Lee Moorehead, former professor of preaching at Saint Paul School of Theology and retired pastor of churches in Illinois and Wisconsin, used to take a poll of his church late in the year, asking, "What are the major issues facing us in the new year?" The responses were tabulated, and then Dr. Moorehead announced to the church that he would preach on the issues that were considered most important by members of the congregation. On the first Sunday of the new year, a short introductory sermon on the number one topic was preached. Then the preacher paused and did some dramatic business. He stepped out of the pulpit, took off his preaching robe, and moved into the midst of the congregation. "Now," he said, "You have heard what I have to say about this issue. What do you have to say?" From that moment on, Dr. Moorehead served as moderator, asking for responses, repeating statements, drawing people out.

When I have used this model, the best parts of the sermon were provided by the congregation. I have learned, however, that this method works best in relatively small congregations where people can hear without amplification and when a large percentage of the members respond. There is more animated participation if the issue is a controversial one.

Another model that includes feedback is provided by O. C. Edwards, Jr. He moves the sermon, feedback session, and eucharist to the parish house. When everyone is comfortably settled, he preaches the sermon and follows that with discussion. "This way the people are relaxed and ready to give themselves to the consideration of the subject. They have the sermon fresh in their minds, they feel no inhibitions about saying their mind, and they have time to do so."[6]

The time of Edward's service is lengthened considerably. The sermon, in Edward's model, is ten to fifteen minutes, and the discussion is thirty to forty-five minutes.

Edwards advocates following the sermon with discussion for several reasons: The preacher discovers whether the congregation understands. Preaching becomes more responsible. The congregation has an obligation to listen. The people will be more deeply committed to the sermon. This model makes it clear that laity, as well as clergy, have spiritual insight.

Another adaptation of the feedback model is to move only the feedback session to another location following the sermon in the sanctuary. Members of the congregation who are interested move to the new location and participate in the feedback. This session may be led by a layperson designated in advance and prepared to lead the discussion. The minister responds only to direct questions.

Such feedback to the sermon trains laity and clergy in attitudes and skills helpful in full participatory preaching. There is a necessary granting of permission to speak that must accompany participatory models. Most people in church have been carefully schooled to sit quietly and speak only when addressed. Persons who have no difficulty talking before and after the service may find it anxiety producing to say anything during worship. In most small membership churches there are opportunities to speak in worship, and these need to be strengthened and expanded.

Telling the Story of the Scripture

"Next Sunday the Gospel lesson is Matthew 26:6-13. The Bible study class is asking everyone to read the lesson in advance. We will read the Gospel as usual next Sunday, but immediately following the reading the congregation will join in retelling the story."

Such an announcement prepares the congregation to participate and creates anticipation. If a study group can make some preparation, that will also be of help. A reader, who may be the minister, reads the story and then invites the people to join in retelling it. An introductory question, such as, "How does the story begin?" may help encourage participation. If the story stalls, the reader may supply the next bit of plot. No one person should monopolize the telling. Such a person may be interrupted with a question for other persons in the congregation. Questions that place the story in context or that ask for additional information about setting, time, or character add interest to the telling. Parallels from other gospels or portions of scripture may also be introduced.

I have asked students to introduce this method of retelling scripture stories. Almost without exception the method has been well received by congregations. Participation has been somewhat more mixed, but never has there been so little participation as to block the retelling. When tested afterward, every congregation has had better retention of the scripture story than the people normally have of scripture readings.

With some practice, small congregations become skilled in retelling scripture stories. For most congregations only a small amount of additional instruction is needed to enable them to move to fully participatory preaching.

Opening or Closing the Sermon

In effect, asking the congregation to assist in retelling the scripture story is a participatory opening of the sermon. Another type of participatory opening is to ask the people to help describe the problem.

Early in the sermon, probably in the first two minutes, the preacher needs to involve the people in a problem or issue involving conflict or tension. If the problem is not experienced by the people, it is doubtful that they will be interested in the answer. How better to get firsthand investment in a real problem than by asking the people to join in its description? The personal nature of the problem can be heightened. Involvement by members of this congregation can be demonstrated. Tension, suspense, conflict, and anticipation are all intensified.

The sermon may be ended in a participatory manner. After the problem has been raised, explored, and a solution discovered, then the people may participate in application to their own lives. "Now, the question is, what can we do? Are there any implications for how we will live our lives this week?"

Since this part of the sermon needs to be somewhat open-ended and all possible applications cannot be explored, why not allow the people to make application to their own lives? This is what preachers want to happen in every sermon. Preachers want each person to wrestle with the issue and find implications for living. In a participatory ending, people can wrestle with implications aloud and so model for others action that is authentic and that represents more than the preacher's conclusions.

Personal Participatory Preaching

This form of preaching is an active dialogic and interpersonal model in which congregational participation is encouraged throughout the sermon.

I shape the sermon after educational and communication theories pioneered by such persons as John Dewey and Alan Monroe. Dewey's "pattern of reflective thinking" revolutionized educational methodology by beginning where the students were and leading them through a series of steps to new insights. This process was adapted by such preachers as Harry Emerson Fosdick and Halford Luccock[7] to perfect a problem-solution style of preaching. Many kinds of preaching have been developed following this direction, including psychological and inductive means of shaping the sermon.

Alan Monroe's "motivated sequence"[8] applies similar principles to communication. His theory begins with identification of a "need" on the part of the audience and leads the listeners through several steps to decision and action.

Although the Dewey and Monroe approaches to communication do careful audience analysis and begin with the problems of the people, they do not make provision for audience participation. Personal participatory preaching utilizes these methods in two ways. It tries to understand the audience's present situation and to use that as a beginning point for communication. It also moves through a sequence designed to bring the congregation to insight. Participation by the congregation forms and corrects the evolving insight. This style of preaching is intended to be personal. The sermon begins from the present, personal perspective of the congregation and deals with issues that have deep personal significance. It is participatory because the preacher needs the help of the congregation in moving from personal issues to personal insight and decision.

A problem, or what Monroe calls a "need," is set up early in the sermon. The people need to both understand and experience this problem. In my practice, the people are given permission to ask questions about this problem, to volunteer personal experiences of the problem, and to discuss its ramifications. Dewey calls this part of the process "defining and limiting the problem." I want the people to experience the problem as one they share. The preacher introduces the problem from both biblical and contemporary sources. The preacher then guides the investigation of the problem with a series of questions, to which the members of the congregation respond. With practice, congregations participate readily. Initially the preacher may need to prepare the congregation for such participation as noted in chapter 2. The preacher guides the development of the need step by step, asking questions such as:

> How does the Bible lesson raise this issue?
> Can you share ways people today face this problem?
> How is this a problem for you?
> Does anyone have personal experience with this problem?
> Are there other aspects of the problem?
> Can we state the problem clearly?

The preacher encourages visualization and dramatiza-
tion of the problem. If no one is able to provide such
images and stories, the preacher should be ready to do so.
Discretely used pastoral material, examples from literature or media, or a personal story may promote such
visualization.

The sermon now turns to possible solutions. The
preacher needs to provide this transition and to encourage
the people to think of various solutions—even if their
solutions are partial and incomplete. This keeps competition from developing between answers. The attitude of the
group should be, "We are trying to find a common answer
together." Additional answers and extensions of answers
are welcome. Dewey evaluates the possible answers. This
must be done with care so no one's contribution is
discarded. Questions by the preacher may continue to guide
the development of the sermon. However, the communication is more conversational than simple question and
answer. The preacher restates or reflects comments. People
in the congregation address one another, and the group
moves together toward solutions.

> How do most people deal with this problem?
> Do some solutions make the problem worse?
> How have you dealt with this issue?
> Are there things we could do to help?
> Are there any biblical answers?

Often in this section of the sermon a preferred answer
(Dewey's term) will be constructed by the group, or a
member will provide such a flash of insight that everyone
recognizes it as a gospel answer. The preacher should
accept this response as the work of the Holy Spirit and not

compete with it. Often biblical resources are brought to complement statements made by individuals.

However, the preacher should be prepared to provide such insight if it is not offered by the congregation. Contributions can be anticipated, and the minister should be prepared to draw them together.

The introduction of a new perspective is an effective way of providing insight. My colleague, Eugene Lowry, calls this "a clue to resolution." "In it one senses the missing key which 'unlocks' the whole. Until found, the matter seems irresolute, after being found, the matter seems self-evident! In gestalt terms, it is the 'aha,' the one piece which allows the whole puzzle to come into sharp focus. Such a revelatory clue is *experienced* by the congregation rather than simply *known*. This enables the whole group to see the problem in a new light that immediately suggests new and better solutions."[9]

Given this new insight, we can turn immediately to implications.

> What does this mean for our lives?
> Can we develop implications for our church?
> What action should we take?

Discussing implications does not need to be a lengthy part of the sermon. Even in a very small group, there will be more consequences for our lives, our church, our community, and our world than we could list. Some samples will do. Again, some person from the group would be encouraged to visualize the action that is required by the solution or new insight.

The Case Study Method of Preaching

Case studies may be used in participatory preaching. The case study method, as used in modern instructional procedures, imports a "real case" and ask the class to study it and then decide what to do under the circumstances described in the case. It is assumed that there is a correct answer. The correct answer is supplied after the class has made its recommendation.

The small congregation is filled with many more "real" cases than the case study method can supply. An indicator of how real these local church cases are is provided by the fact that there are seldom "correct" answers to prescribe. The case (I don't like the word *case;* I prefer *pastoral occasion*) that began this chapter was too alive to be written down, mimeographed, and distributed. It happened only once. Likewise, the help given in the service was much more than verbal. Direction was given, not definitive and complete answers. I recommend a pastoral use of the case method in which people empathize with the situation described and discuss options.

Care should be taken to protect the confidence of any person who has brought personal problems to the minister. Pastoral occasions from the minister's counseling should not be used unless there is full agreement on the part of the person or persons involved. Also, the minister should be careful not to use people or pressure them to reveal more than they want to share in church. However, the minister's reticence may be due not to ethical procedure but to hestiancy about dealing with the life issues of the community. In the small church, everyone may already know the story. The minister's reluctance to use the case may be a desire to avoid difficult issues. Dealing with sensitive personal issues in the gathered community is good pastoral care. Such care meets the needs of both the individual and the community.

Helen asks whether the church has any ritual for divorce. Her marriage with John has ended. The minister also knows that the congregation is puzzled and has difficulty knowing how to handle the divorce. The wedding was a big celebration in the church. It doesn't seem right to ignore the new situation created by their divorce. Helen and the minister decide to deal with the case in a sermon.

Helen can't talk when the sermon begins. John's parents are in the circle with their mouths set in a disapproving line. Their silence reminds Helen of the alienation she feels from her own parents—and she still loves John's parents. John and Helen's marriage had held such promise. They were two kids in the community who grew up together. They had "gone steady" all through high school, and had spent years in this circle holding hands. The hopes nurtured in a small church die hard.

"How can I come back to church," she asks, "when everyone here thinks of me as part of John?"

"If we can't work it out here in the family, where can we deal with it?" Jeff asks.

We seem set up for rebuke and recrimination until Uncle Raymond says, "I still love Helen and John whether they're divorced or not."

May adds, "Well, I still don't believe in divorce, but there's a lot of things I don't favor that happen. Helen, I'm going to help you all I can."

The preacher finally suggests two prayers: a prayer of confession of broken relationships and a prayer asking for strength for Helen in her new state. Everyone joins in both prayers and in the hugs afterward.

Case studies can be of great help in participatory preaching at two points. First, cases portray problems as genuine, local, and afflicting people like us. Many problems described in sermons are too easy—designed to set up situations in which the preacher can provide ready answers. However, when someone in the congregation brings his or her own problem, it has authenticity and immediacy. When people trust the group, they are often willing to bring personal problems to the group to find help. It should be noted, however, that the group and the minister must be sensitive to the person. Deep probing is generally inappropriate. The problems don't have to be cases of baring one's soul. Often minor events in a person's life may point to an issue that needs attention in this group.

The second time where personal experience can be helpful in the sermon is at the point when the group is looking for solutions. Statements like "How I dealt with this in my own life . . ." are helpful. Again, the minister must exercise care to see that sensitivity is used. Some personal experiences will not be helpful in finding gospel solutions. The right witness at the right time can be a powerful means of bringing the congregation to the gospel moment.

Preparation for Participatory Preaching

We have looked at involving the people in preparation for preaching in chapter 2. What preparation must the preacher make?

A different kind of preparation is required for participatory preaching than for standard sermons. The standard sermon places the preacher in control. The selection and sequencing of material is determined by the preacher, and the preacher has only to answer questions that he or she raises.

Exegesis of scripture is a familiar kind of preparation for any preaching, but it is particularly important in participatory preaching. General hemeneutical principles are more likely to be questioned and examined by the congregation. The preacher needs to be intentional and open about methods used. The preacher should also be clear about laying a solid exegetical base before moving into imaginative extensions. Historical criticism can prepare the preacher to examine the textual setting, time, characters, and events; this is the stuff of narrative and demonstrates the close relationship between exegesis and story. Almost certainly the congregation will speculate about twentieth-century extensions and expressions. Modern settings and character traits will be supplied— "What would happen today?" This extension can be the ally of exegesis, rather than it's enemy, if the work of exegesis is kept primary. Redaction criticism studies the text, additions, and clues to the intention of the original author and subsequent editors. As the modern congregation tries to come to consensus concerning God's will for our time, the preacher needs an accurate understanding of the theology of the text.

Participatory preaching gives attention to the shape of the sermon and the sequence that will be followed. Questions, resources, visualization, clues to resolution, and application all need preparation. The sermon will not be preached in the standard verbal form. The participatory model may range into unexpected territory. The preacher needs to prepare for surprises.

A major part of preparation in this model is learning to call forth the resoures of the community. Insight into the needs of people in the congregation and some anticipation of the expression of needs is helpful. Think about the direction solutions are likely to take. Who has some experiences that illuminate others?

The Role of the Preacher

When the sermon belongs only to the preacher, it tends to become a "thing," measured in minutes rather than in human experience. If the preacher is not a member of the extended family, the sermon comes from another world. If there is no participation by the people, the sermon is required as something good the church needs to be healthy, but it is generally taken like medicine.

When the sermon belongs to the people, it is a happening that gives expression and significance to the relationship between God and these folks. Such a sermon celebrates who the people are and shapes who they are becoming. It brings health to the church as exercise brings health to the body. The preacher is a member of and speaks in the accents of the family. The preacher doesn't need to speak all the time; it's important to listen. The role is often to help other people speak. "Relationships are more likely to be furthered by an interested listener than by an engaging talker."[10]

There is a temptation to regard the proclamation of the Word as the exclusive preserve of the clergy. If a word needs to be spoken on behalf of the church; if the dominant culture should be called to accountability; if the evangel needs to be proclaimed, the church turns to the ministers. Proclamation is compressed into one weekly sermon, and the congregation assumes no further responsibility.

It would help to right this imbalance and remind the whole church of its ministry if we had a style of preaching that shared the important work of witnessing between clergy and laity. Participatory preaching involves both preacher and people in speaking the proclamation, gives both a sense of investment in the event of preaching, and commissions both to ministry. Carl Braaten, at the end of his book *The Apostolic Imperative*, says that "church work" for laity is narrowly defined as giving money or doing committee work. "The challenge," he says, "is not to help the laity to get tuned in on the church's monolog, but to prepare them for dialog and even confrontation with the powers at play in their secular callings."[11]

Delivery and *performance* describe the style of conventional preaching. Recently these words have been supplemented by such words as *conversational* and *dialogical*. The first set of words places emphasis on the speaker and what the speaker does. They are subjectively oriented: "I" deliver (distribute, give). "I" perform (carry out, do). *Conversation* and *dialogue* place emphasis on an exchange or a transaction. They are relational words: "We" converse (exchange thoughts). "We" participate in dialogue.

Participatory preaching builds on this relational emphasis in modern preaching and takes it a step further. Instead of simulating dialogue, participatory preaching enters into actual verbal transaction with the congregation. The communication doesn't just give the appearance of being two-way—it is. The receivers of the message not only take in, but they also become senders and participate in a spiral of communication, where messages are exchanged, checked, and transmuted into new forms no one could produce alone. Delivery is a vehicle for communication. It also signals and supports a personal, caring relationship. Personal participatory preaching is marked by the following.

Identification with the congregation. Respect for members of the congregation is matched by an ability to make people feel accepted. Their needs are understood, and their comments are welcomed. The preacher is sensitive to the feelings of the people. This style requires that the preacher know what is happening in people's minds and emotions and between members of the congregation.

Trust. Authenticity is always important, and it is especially so in participatory preaching. Ethos, credibility, and trustworthiness as developed in all relationships come to prominence in preaching.

Dialogue. The preacher engages the people in conversation. A stimulating style, ability to involve others, and skill at drawing out contributions all mark conversational delivery. Conversation does not refer to careless and indifferent speaking. It refers to the exchange of ideas with keen and insightful urgency. Drama, change of pace, and rhetorical methods generally are useful in conversation.

Guidance. A sense of direction is fixed, and the sermon is ordered according to a determined sequence. The preacher may rephrase, supplement, question, link comments, and move the discussion along. Occasionally it will be necessary to bring the conversation back to the sequence. Timing—knowing when to pause and reflect and when to quicken the tempo—is important.

Personal address. The ability to close distance, to speak caringly and directly, and to create the intimate moment are critical skills. In this setting, the preacher can literally move toward a person or put a hand on someone's arm. The voice can be lowered. This personal quality is communicated through the group, and everyone becomes more caring and attentive. The congregation develops empathy—particularly sensitivity to hurt, confusion, and frustration.

Rapid analysis. The preacher must manage the turns in the narrative, catch the significance of contributions, otherwise lost in verbiage, anticipate the climax, and summarize clearly.

Mediation of disagremeents. Insight into the extent and nature of differences will help the group establish common ground. Discussion of differences of opinion is helpful as members try to determine where they stand. Some reflection of feelings as well as ideas will enable members to monitor their own emotional intensity. The preacher occasionally must serve as objective referee as members work out disagreements.

Theological perspective. Biblical and historical resources are marshaled. Theological method informs the sermon. The preacher supplies a Christian perspective and is able to gather the sermon into a coherent whole. Conflict in the narrative is made personal and of moment. The clue to resolution comes as a great discovery. Implications apply concretely. The preacher needs a stimulating conviction that the sermon matters.

Competency. The preacher should refrain from doing the people's work for them. The group wrestles with problems and gropes for solutions. Some members will want the preacher to reach conclusions for them. The result is unwarranted generalizations or pious clichés. People can work out their own implications and the community can come to consensus if the preacher is not too ready to tell them what to do.

The role of the preacher is not made easier or less important by lay participation. The people are taken inside the preacher's workshop and are encouraged to make preparation for the sermon by studying the scripture lessons. This results in more Bible study by both the clergy and the laity. The preacher's role in delivery is changed, but not lessened. People are encouraged to share, but it is the preacher who must enable this sharing. The preacher can anticipate some development, but will find it necessary to make preparation along several lines rather than for just one sequence. The preacher may not write a sermon manuscript. Instead, questions follow a narrative outline. The preacher prepares essential parts of the sermon and is ready to deliver them as needed.

The Role of the People

Participation is not a gimmick or just an added dimension. It is essential to this style of preaching. Participation is important in itself, but it also adds important content and dynamics. It takes place in and adds to the liturgical and theological context. It helps define the nature of the church. This is a worshiping and witnessing congregation. There is an informing *kerygma*, a preaching of God's act in Jesus Christ by the whole people of God.

Laity are accustomed to taking active roles in the small church. A large percentage of the people take an active role in the worship service—greeting, passing out hymnals, playing the piano and performing other music, leading the singing, praying, reading, making announcements, raising concerns, and so on. There is a high sense of investment in the service. Often members feel that they will be missed if they are absent because their contribution is needed.

Occasionally, people express a hesitancy to add or participate in the sermon because it is "God's Word." I want to affirm that high estimate of preaching while encouraging a broadening of participation. How can people feel that the sermon is the Word of God while they are participating in it? The same way ministers do. This hesitancy probably results more from what preachers have taught concerning role differentiation than it does from personal experiences of the laity. The priesthood of all believers is still an important doctrine in small churches. Member participation in acts of worship tends to validate God's presence rather than hinder it. The same should be true for the sermon.

Personal participatory preaching as set out in this chapter is an introduction to the several styles offered in this book. The preacher and the congregation should be flexible in their use. The method may turn highly pastoral as in the example at the beginning of this chapter. Sometimes participatory preaching will emphasize Bible study. Other times this kind of preaching will bring the congregation to decision making, as in chapter 5. Whatever shape is given to this style of preaching, it requires that both the preacher and the people trust God to guide the sermon and make it helpful and relevant on any particular Sunday.

4

Participatory Biblical Narrative Preaching

The small church shares stories. Members of the group are familiar with the family background of persons present. They were present to mark important passages in the lives of members. Episodes in their lives are remembered and retold. Often anecdotes about one another are shared as the common possession of the community. When the group gathers, it shares a body of oral tradition. This oral tradition is told in story form often enough to keep it fresh in the corporate memory. In contrast, most large congregations have no such repository of oral tradition; members of the large church often know little about one another. Not only is there a repository of story in the small church, but also members customarily tell these stories. A few members of the small community may develop special skills and become known as storytellers. They conserve and pass on these memories. Storytellers serve as preservers of the traditions of the community. When a person of the church is named, the people hold a body of anecdotes in their minds that help them come to an estimate of the character of that person. Persons are linked with families and so share in a larger treasury of stories. Important times and particular places are woven into the oral tradition. The community itself comes to have a story in which all the members share. The members receive an important part of their identity by being linked to the story of the group.

A role of liturgy (formal and informal) in the small church is the retelling of the corporate story. Members of the community know who they are because they are linked in their own minds and in the minds of their associates with the corporate story. Storytelling is more than casual entertainment. The remembering of stories is a way of being constituted. Stories participate in the events they chronicle. They are sacramental. The remembering they represent is what sacramental theology calls *anamnesis*. *Anamnesis* is a Greek word often translated as "remember." The English usage fails to translate a critical factor. *Anamnesis* also makes present and available the thing or person that is remembered. That is the role of storytelling in the small church. When the story is told, it *re*members. The happening is put together again for us today so that we live it again. The hearer becomes a participant. Memory tapes are activated. Time, as well as space, is suspended, and the familiar characters from the past are present as the story is told.

Remembrance becomes even more significant when it becomes a corporate experience enabling the community to rehearse its common memories. Israelites recalled the "mighty acts" of God. They reminded themselves that they were a "chosen people," "led out of Egypt," and "children of Abraham, Isaac, and Jacob." Such memory altered the present and made those who were remembered part of those who kept the recollection alive. A *mezuzah* on a doorpost, a pillar raised in the desert, a meal kept by faithful disciples had the potential of bringing the past into the present. Stripped of such recourse to memory, there is no way for us to know who we are. Biblical usage assumes a particular quality in life that can be maintained only by remembrance. This is the quality of buoyant faith. A poet in the book of Jonah witnesses, "When my soul fainted within me, I remembered the Lord" (Jon. 2:7). A preacher in the early Christian community says, "I think it right . . . to arouse you by way of reminder" (II Pet. 1:13). Memory revives faith and enables it to grow. The Holy Spirit moves among us, utilizing memory. The holiest act of the Christian faith is instituted and marked by the words, "Do this in remembrance *(anamnesis)* of me." The small church recognizes and uses memory in this way because it is a common way of recollecting life experiences.

Story and sacrament are defined in terms of participation. This is participation at two levels: our own personal investment and the participation of God.

Story and sacrament tell and act the event of God's coming to us. It is the story of God living, forgiving, and empowering—centered in the incarnation. It becomes gospel when the catalyst is applied that causes the old stories and the old rituals to interact with our contemporary lives. It is not the gospel until it becomes the gospel for *us*. In that process, our hurts are compared to the hurts of other people in other times. Universal stories and rituals of hurt and healing become existential. Each person experiences the hurt and begins to share in the healing. Inclusion in the story brings about healing.

This is why biblical narrative is so important in the small church. In many small congregations, members are able to remember and to tell stories of individuals and of the community. They are accustomed to reliving their stories. The biblical stories have often entered the pool of interpretive stories so that the people understand themselves in terms of the biblical stories. Sam Keen in *To a Dancing God*[1] remembers that though he had grown up in Tennessee he understood the geography of Palestine much better than he did that of his home state. The biblical stories in Keen's childhood were much more interpretive for him than were the stories of Tennessee.

It is natural in many small churches to move into a biblical story with the expectation it will reveal significant insight into our modern lives—help us to know who we are and what kind of lives we should live. Another way of saying this is that our stories in the small group are connected to The Story. The story is God's action on our behalf that gives meaning to our lives and promise of salvation.

The vehicle for The Story is the Bible. The Bible is so valued in many small churches that there is identification between Bible and Story. The heat generated in defense of the Bible indicates that something more is at stake than a doctrine of inspiration. It is really The Story that is being defended—that which gives meaning and promise of salvation to our lives. Sometimes this may be called the Word, and a distinction is drawn between the written Word and the active Word. In the small church, that explanation is more likely to be heard if the distinction is drawn between Bible and Story.

Study of the Bible is central to preaching. Historically, sermons have had texts. These texts supplied authority as well as content. Therefore, study of the biblical text is normative. Whatever method of preaching is used, there should be solid exegetical study behind it. That is particularly true of participatory styles of preaching, where the preacher does not decide what exegesis to include and what to exclude. The group may need more

and different exegetical help than the preacher anticipated. This exegesis may be a shared endeavor. Significant
Christian education occurs when a minister is willing to
share exegetical methodology with members of the
congregation and to guide them in its use. Good exegesis
can take the congregation into the world of the passage
and help link them to their own stories. Participatory
exegesis can teach the congregation more about the Bible
and its study in a few weeks than they may learn in years
of conventional preaching. This kind of preaching is not
just Bible study. It must move on to have an impact on the
lives of the participants.

> Biblical preaching from the New Testament is, by
> definition, the task of bringing about an encounter
> between people of the twentieth century and the Word of
> God—first spoken in the first century. The task of exegesis
> is to discover that Word and its meaning in the first
> century church: the task of preaching is to know well *both*
> the exegesis of the text *and* the people to whom that Word
> is now to be spoken again, as a living Word for them.[2]

Much of the Bible is in narrative form, and narrative lies
behind much of the rest. From the sagas of Genesis to the
parables of Jesus, narrative has been the preferred vehicle
for revelation. Biblical narrative grounds and shapes the
style of participatory preaching in this chapter.

"The story" is central to this style of preaching. It is this
story that provides the unity of the New Testament. The
controversy over unity and diversity in the New Testament
represents two correct opinions. The unity the story gives
to the New Testament is not one of agreement of historical
recounting, shared opinion, or certainly not infallible
reporting. It is one of viewpoint. There is diversity of turns

in plot, disagreement about detail, and various interpre-
tations. *Faith* is the word most often used to denote the
peculiar viewpoint that unifies the whole and sees in the
story line God's own revelation. It is "the event which
makes all other events intelligible."[3] Faith is the
perspective that this biblical story will give meaning to
our lives. Finally, as Reynolds Price says in his introduction
to Rhoads and Michie's *Mark as Story:* "How a believer in
Mark's tale is expected to behave in the remainder of his
daily life is left bracingly but frighteningly to the believer's
own deduction and invention."[4]

The story, therefore, is open. Each reader or hearer
must complete it in his or her own time. Exegesis must
always lead to interpretation. It should admit from the
beginning that it is a faith statement. A community
struggling together not only to understand the original
statement of the story, but also to give it expression in
their own lives is the truest exegete of all.

Participatory biblical narrative preaching is therefore
placed in two contexts. The first context is the biblical
narrative that finally draws on the whole biblical canon.
The most appropriate way to proceed with this kind of
preaching is to choose a holistic and comprehensive
lectionary (like the three year common lectionary) and
gradually be exposed to the whole canon. This is best
illustrated in the Gospel lesson, where Sunday by Sunday
the community hears the story in order and is given a
sense of the whole Gospel context. I particularly like the
Psalm–Passion Sunday dramatic reading, where the
whole Passion narrative is read. The congregation needs
occasions when they hear, if not the whole story, a whole
substory. I wonder if other parts of the narrative couldn't

be given such a dramatic statement at other times during the year.

Second, the context of the contemporary community is also important. This small group of dependable people work through the story for themselves so that the narrative begins to have a dénouement in this setting, for these people.

The Relationship of Story and Stories

Biblical narrative preaching tries to tell several stories at the same time. The story of the scripture passage is the presenting vehicle, and its plot will provide the sequence or shape of the sermon. The congregation retells the conflict of the presenting story, deepening and complicating it with introduction of characterization, setting, and further turns in the plot. The group brings the sermon to a high level of frustration, as there seems to be no way out of the labyrinth created. Suddenly, the group seizes on a minor theme that has played almost unobserved through the early telling of the story. It may be turning the problem over and looking at it in a different way. A new perspective provides fresh insight or another direction. The group tests and tries this new and exciting possibility until the story takes off in another direction—toward resolution and fulfillment.

While the presenting story is being told, a second, more primary *story* accompanies it. *The story* provides necessary theological framework for the presenting story. *The story* (gospel, *kerygma*, Word) informs the conflict with a fuller understanding of the human predicament. The gracefulness of *the story* provides the climate for and the clue to resolution. No one passage can supply *the story*;

stories provide occasions for application of *the story*. The group must learn not to shackle themselves with too inflexible a literalism in retelling the presenting story and to leave room for *the story* to correct and to extend the presenting story. Individual presenting narratives will often be deficient in Christology, particularly soteriology, but the group has recourse to *the story*—the whole biblical gospel—in the telling of stories.

A third story, or group of stories, is that of the people participating in the sermon. As we have seen, the small church is aware of the stories of members, of the inter-relationship of members' stories, and of how these coalesce into a corporate story. The presenting story has a historic setting, conflict, and characters. As this presenting story is told, a second narrative line begins to form alongside the original plot. This second narrative line is a viewing of the historic setting, conflict, and characters in terms of our contemporary setting, conflict, and plot.

Any preaching involves interpretation. We need to be intentional about exegetical responsibility. The historic situation should be reported as accurately as possible. However, we admit, even with the best exegetical methodology we always see the ancient material through modern eyes. This may be the frustration of the exegete, but it is the glory of the preacher. As the people tell the historic story, they begin to compare the setting to the place they live—how is Gadara like East Branch? Characters are understood in terms of ourselves and the people we know. The conflicts and problems of ancient times look surprisingly like our own. This participating story, gleaned from our own situations, is essential to preaching.

In conventional preaching, the minister must supply this contemporary, participating story from his or her own life and knowledge of the lives of people in the parish. A strength of participatory preaching is that the people tell their own stories, draw their own comparisons, and adjust the presenting and participating stories.

The role of the preacher is to guide and enable the preaching of the sermon so that the presenting story, *the story*, and the participating stories of the people all get told. The preacher draws out the members of the congregation so that they take their essential role in the preaching of the sermon. This is a creative process.

Note that I don't say that the preacher is to control the group. Controlling factors—such as an authoritarian preacher or an inflexible interpretation of the text—defeat creativity. Congregations within themselves generally underestimate their creative ability. They will probably overestimate the lack of an enabling climate. It is true that the congregation needs to cultivate its ability to risk, and members can help preach the sermon better if they are willing to be vulnerable to one another. However, the uptight, divided, and distrustful congregation often discovers a wonderful thing happening as the narrative line begins to take shape. In spite of themselves, the story line elicits self-disclosure. Dialogue stimulates further dialogue. People begin to trust one another with their stories. The church discovers that it stands in a tradition of grace more resilient than local acrimony.

This is first experienced as members investigate the conflict in the presenting story and the "hurt" that their participating stories add. Often people show sensitivity and caring in their descriptions of "what is wrong." Even as they deepen the problem by making it personal and more complicated, they begin to realize that it is a problem they share. In preparation groups and in the

Sunday morning telling of the story, I encourage the group to "dig the pit deeper than you can climb out of." When the historical conflict is told, it introduces a serious problem to the group. When people add their own experiences of the problem, it becomes unmanageable. When it is linked to the human predicament, the hurt is both personal and universal and threatens to inundate us. It is then that the church has the opportunity and necessity of becoming the universal church. The members of the congregation have been willing to plumb the depths of despair together. Now they can experience the grace of God together. Discovery is exhilarating. Discovering a graceful alternative to a pressing hurt is the ultimate sermonic experience. It also creates the situation in which the small church can be a sign of God's continuing graceful presence in our midst.

A sample of biblical narrative preaching may help us gain a feel for the method.

Preacher: Today the sermon will be a participatory biblical narrative. You are invited to join with me in telling the story of the rich young ruler. Three persons are prepared to read the different lessons. These accounts are found in Mark 10:17-31, Matthew 19:16-30, and Luke 18:18-30. Listen with special care, for we want to be true to the scriptural record. I also encourage you to use your imagination in order to fill in parts of the story not included in the *Gospels*. (The scripture passages are read.) You have heard three accounts of the story of the Rich Young Ruler. Just before this event, Jesus and the disciples leave Galilee and turn south toward Jerusalem. What time of day do you think it was?

Response: They were just getting started, but I think it was late morning because the disciples were slow moving.

Preacher: Why was that?

Response: They weren't anxious to get on toward Jerusalem. They were unsure what was going to happen.

Response: Strange things were happening, and there was serious opposition.

Preacher: Then the setting is one of apprehension and uncertainty?

Response: If I were going to stage it today, I'd have a thunderstorm coming up.

Preacher: Then what happened?

Response: A young man came elbowing his way through the crowd to talk to Jesus.

Preacher: "Elbowing his way," you say. What kind of man is he?

Response: Well, he's rich. He has on fine clothes.

Response: He has a certain bearing—he expects people to step aside for him and listen to him.

Response: He's young, too. He must have come from a good family to have wealth so soon.

Response: I think he's a Type A personality. He's a real pusher—anxious to get things done.

Preacher: What does he want?

Response: Eternal life. He wants to know what he has to do to have eternal life.

Preacher: All the Gospels call him rich. Matthew calls him young, and Luke calls him a ruler. Why would such a man be hounded by the question of eternal life?

(pause)

Response: Because he wasn't at peace with himself.

Response: Because he wasn't satisfied with what he had—or, maybe, with what he was making of life.

Preacher: Why was that?

Response: Well, there are times when you try to do the right thing and be the right kind of person—the kind that keeps all the commandments—and still there doesn't seem to be much meaning to life.

Preacher: Tell me his story.

Response: He had been expected to be a good boy and take over the family business from the day he was born. He tried hard to live up to everyone's expectations.

Reseponse: Maybe he didn't like that much responsibility.

Preacher: He felt caught?

Response: He just wanted to be alone in a little shop and make fine furniture with his own hands.

Response: Or, maybe, he just wanted to be a disciple of some simple, good man.

Preacher: And then one day such a man appeared in the next village and came walking down the path toward the rich young ruler's own town.

Response: And the young man wanted more than anything to leave everything and go with Jesus.

Preacher: The rich young ruler knew that even before Jesus arrived?

Response: Yes, I think so.

Response: And he also knew that he couldn't go.

Preacher: Then the demand that Jesus made of him wasn't so unreasonable after all?

Response: Oh, it was unreasonable enough, but it was the same demand his family made of him and his business made of him and his ruling class made of him.

Response: Give up everything and follow me.

Preacher: Why is it that Jesus asks such hard questions of the young man?

Response: He wants to get inside the young man, to find out what sort of person he is.

Response: I think there was an edge to the young man's reply about keeping the commandments.

Preacher: Mark portrays Jesus as offering a kind of salvation that can't be gotten by keeping the commandments.

Response: The young man has tried that and knows that there is more to salvation than obedience.

Preacher: Is it possible that the final demand, "Give up everything and follow me," is really good news rather than a demand for obedience?

Response: It sounds like another commandment, but . . .

Response: "Come follow me," is a new liberty.

Response: There have been times when I wanted just to ditch it all—give it all up and go off somewhere.

Preacher: Was Jesus' invitation too simple an answer?

Response: The young man thought so, and he was sad that he couldn't go.

Preacher: I agree. It is a strange kind of invitation, but there is one more reason for Jesus' speaking to the young man as he did. I couldn't understand Jesus at first. I could understand the rich young ruler better. Then I looked at Jesus from a different perspective and saw something that makes all the difference. The lesson begins, "As he was setting out on a journey. . . ." Suddenly, I thought, "He's setting out on a journey from which he will not return." Later in the chapter Jesus tells the disciples that he is going to be arrested and killed. Suddenly Jesus' behavior in this story begins to make sense. He is not inviting the young man to go on just another journey. He is inviting him, in Bonhoeffer's words, to "Come and die." The cross is in the background. The cross Jesus talks about a few verses later puts everything in a different light. It's like the Trapp family fleeing Nazi rule in Austria. They leave houses and fortune and flee over the mountains. It's like the person given three months to live—suddenly everything can be given away. This is not a story to enforce keeping the commandments or even to recommend commitment to Jesus. It is basic gospel. To follow Jesus is to go to a cross. Only beyond that is the man's quest satisfied—eternal life. What happens next?

Response: The rich young ruler goes away.

Preacher: Where is he going?

Response: I don't know, but Jesus loved him.

Preacher: That should be enough.

Response: Maybe he was going home to the business to be a disciple in a different way.

Preacher: Why is he sad?

Response: He may know more about where Jesus is going than any of the others.

Preacher: Are there any implications for us in this story?

Response: The only way to find eternal life wherever we live our lives is at the foot of the cross.

Delivery and Helping People to Share

The "caughtness" of the rich young ruler in the sermon above is supplied and extended out of the participating stories of the community.

One of the respondents says, "There are times when you try to do the right thing and be the right kind of person—the kind that keeps all commandments—and still there doesn't seem to be much meaning to life."

The people in the congregation knew this statement was authentic. They recognized it as coming out of the consciousness of a person who felt that way about himself. The whole sequence describing the situation of the rich young ruler was operating at a second level, a level of insight into the feelings of a member of the community. Suddenly the congregation could understand the rich young ruler better because they were coming to understand a member of the family better.

Later, the same person in the group said, "There have been times when I wanted to ditch it all, give it all up and go off somewhere."

The rich young ruler, as characterized in this sermon, helps a man in the congregation to understand himself. This modern hearer comes to understand that the call to follow Jesus is not an easy way out. Sometimes it is an invitation to stay home and take care of the family business.

About this time, preachers are beginning to suspect that the participatory biblical narrative sermon is a different kind of preaching.

"Everything I knew about preaching just went out the window!"

That's a slight exaggeration, but this kind of preaching does require new skills. Most preachers have acquired storytelling skills in recent years, but the addition of the participation of the congregation adds a new dimension.

I will not review the whole subject of storytelling, but I will add some special help for the preacher who wants to involve the people in the telling. This builds on what I said about delivery in chapter 3 and addresses the particular delivery of narrative.

The beginning is important. Hooks and gimmicks to get attention at the beginning are the stock-in-trade of the storyteller. The preacher who assumes that the congregation is a captive audience loses most of the people before the first paragraph is finished. The opening needs to be jarring, have compelling human interest, or ask a question that can't be dodged. Less often than after dinner speakers suppose, humor will work.

Whatever precedes the story colors the opening. For the biblical narrative what precedes the story is most often the reading of the lesson. It is mumbled, yawned, or read with frozen indifference in most churches. The attempt to loosen a live story from this embalmed lesson reminds preachers why Jesus wept before he tried to resuscitate Lazarus.

Whoever reads the scripture, lay or clergy, should have good skills in oral interpretation. It doesn't have to be a polished radio announcer with resonating chambers in all the bones, but it does have to be someone who cares about the story and the congregation and who can introduce one to the other.

The best stories begin with conflict. Great literature can spend chapters delineating character and describing setting. Sermons are more like popular fiction. The formula is to start the conflict on the first page.

Detective story: Begin with at least one corpse.

Gothic romance: Throw her into his arms and snatch her away immediately.

Western: Bring the horse home with blood on the saddle.

Spy potboiler: Betray the nation and compromise the spy before the reader is settled in.

Look for the conflict. Involve people in the conflict as soon as possible. Find a way for them to explain how this problem feels because they have experienced it themselves.

Conflict is too narrow a word. Suspense, ambiguity, anxiety, and tension all contain something to add to the definition. The congregation must be arrested and caused to open an issue that demands to be closed again where no closure is readily available. Set their minds to asking impossible questions, to experiencing loss of control, and to seeking something just out of reach. Introduce the conflict, and then invite the congregation to deepen and personalize it. If this essential action of the plot has carried the members of the congregation with it, they will respond readily.

The story can be interrupted or advanced. The conventional sermon moves on to the next point when the prior material is used up. It doesn't determine when the time is right or the people are ready. One of the most difficult things to teach preachers is how to stay in touch with the congregation. The preacher should not continue with the sermon until the people have experienced the last thing that happened in the story. Don't move on to resolution until the congregation has experienced the conflict. It doesn't matter what the notes or manuscript say. The manuscript may have too much or too little. In either case, it is wrong and should not be followed. The congregation must be heeded. Has the congregation understood? Have they experienced? The advantage of participatory preaching is that the congregation tells the preacher and one another whether or not they have experienced the conflict. The congregation responds in conventional preaching, too, but it is easier to ignore. Some preachers will get through the manuscript as they planned, regardless of signs from the congregation. A great gray curtain seems to fall down between the pulpit and the pews. The preacher completes the manuscript even if the congregation files quietly out. In storytelling, it is essential that the preacher and the people move together through the sequence of the plot. Participatory preaching helps that to happen.

Interruptions in participatory preaching are not to be ignored as irritating blockages of the preacher's intention. What has seemed an interruption to me has often represented the congregation well. Sometimes the "interruption" has developed into a major contribution to the sermon. Let's say you were right and the comment is wide of the mark, an interruption. It may not just interrupt; it may threaten to take everyone off in a wrong direction. It is a sign. It means that at least one person, and maybe several, have lost the narrative line. The preacher needs to rehearse or recapitulate and engage everyone with the flow again.

Advancing comments generally do not need help from the preacher. The preacher doesn't have to say it all. If a comment advances the story, stay out of its way. Others will pick it up and continue with the story. If the group is too large for everyone to hear, then some restatement may be necessary. If the advancing comment is by a participant who has been shy, then some appreciative use of the comment may be in order. Generally, encourage advancing the story by moving on.

Tempo and timing are supplied by the preacher and caught by the congregation. Some parts of the sermon are reflective and thoughtful. There are pauses and questions during this part of the story. It moves deliberately. Other material moves rapidly. This nimble material may be inconsequential information, or it may move with legerity because it is momentous. Sometimes, an anticipation of the climax causes the story to rush on. There is a symbiotic relationship when the story catches on, and the preacher and the people move together with a common tempo.

The alert preacher occasionally interrupts the flow intentionally for dramatic purpose. Sometimes it is necessary to raise a hand, pause, and ask an unexpected question or take a surprising turn in direction. This dramatic timing is especially apt as the story approaches the climax. Climaxes need to be anticipated, but not predictable. Jesus' parables grew out of the common world of the hearers, but their climaxes were so surprising that the congregation was left gasping. We have drained them of all their stored exclamations by our conventional use, but the original telling left people dumbfounded.

Conventional preaching marshals evidence until a predictable conclusion is supported and recommended. Biblical narrative sometimes retells a story the people know, and the end of the story is anticipated and told with satisfaction. The best use of biblical narrative, however, has a means of restoring the unanticipated quality of the first telling. In these sermons, the climax comes as an "aha." This can be done with familiar stories and usually involves a change of perspective or an introduction of another viewpoint. A contemporary setting or introduction of modern characters may be all that is needed—the parable of the workers in the vineyard may become a story about a modern labor union. Participation by the congregation adds a contemporaneity that makes old stories fresh and new. Picking up a minor or overlooked part of a biblical story results in a new hearing of the story. The idea that Jesus invited the rich young ruler to "follow me" on a journey from which they would not return provides a new way for considering the invitation.

Surprises come from the congregation. The unexpected and graceful insight may be supplied when the preacher had thought to make a modest point. The gospel is like that. If the gospel is to be well represented in the sermon, a dramatic statement is needed. Sermons spend a disproportionate amount of time analyzing the situation or heightening consciousness. Save a little time for celebration.

Skill in interviewing is helpful. Asking good questions moves the story along. We have all heard interviews in which the questions could be answered with monosylla-bles—no, yes, and so on. The skilled interviewer elicits not only information, but also a rich fabric of feeling, hopes, fears, and imaginative stories. It can be the difference between plodding through an old story and having a new, life-changing experience.

Again, the small church gathers. Prepared in advance, members expect to participate in the sermon. The biblical lessons provide the agenda. Questions by the preacher follow the narrative development of the passage and encourage the group to fill out the story. There are questions about setting, time, and place. Discussion enables the congregation to provide more detail about the characters. Questions about plot follow: What are the turns in the story? Why do these things happen? Dialogue examines conflict, feeling, and intention. The discussion follows the sequence of the story. The tempo quickens as the story approaches the climax. The preacher wraps up the story with a surprising and gospel-oriented word. The congregation responds with a few applications and implications. Finally the congregation sings and prays. Still they stand around talking, resisting leaving a community that has told their story one more time.

CHAPTER

5

Participatory Preaching and Decision Making

Many sermons are followed by an unspoken question, "So what?" Spoken and unspoken questions continue to rumble after the sermon. The most devastating questions are "So what?"; "What difference does it make?"; and "What does it matter?"

Insouciance grips much of modern preaching. There is no intimation that momentous issues hang in the balance. It's business as usual. The sermon seems designed to fill only twenty minutes.

The congregation files out languidly with no action in mind. The church will initiate no new programs as a result of this sermon. Another sermon has been put quietly to rest; it will have no continued life in the church.

Not every sermon can be Paul's proclamation on Mars Hill or John Wesley's field preaching to the Bristol miners. However, the congregation does deserve to have its time put to good use. Preacher and congregation should be convinced that it matters.

The sermon may have ideas enough. It may deal with issues that command the attention of the people, but the ideas and issues are dismantled at the end. Concluding words merely restate or summarize, and the preacher ends with bootless resignation. No decision is called for. No action is incited.

That's not the way with New Testament preaching. The New Testament prophets picture a God who demands response. Sermons in that tradition deserve vivifying and psyche rattling endings. The form of preaching in this chapter asks the congregation not only to respond during the sermon, but also to move to decision.

I ask preachers to prepare sermons with a response in mind. Preaching is to be taken out of isolation, out of the solitude of the preacher's study, and thrown into the arena of the community. The whole congregation must become responsive.

When a sermon is recorded or printed, it ceases to be a sermon and becomes a dead reminder of a lived moment. This death occurs, it seems obvious, because the sermon is wrenched away from the living person who spoke it. That is only part of the truth. What robs it of life is that it is torn out of relationship. It is not the preacher alone who makes the sermon. It is community property. The life of the group is the necessary context for preaching. The group calls forth the sermon and adds to preaching of the eternal Word a necessary contemporary expression. The word is not the Word until it is received in a specific and fresh context. Response is a constitutive element.

Great preachers and their sermons model much from which we can learn. However, emphasis needs to be placed on the original community that heard the sermon. If we better understood the dynamics of the relationship between preacher and community, we might select different preachers and sermons for study.

The relationship between preacher and responsive community is central in preaching. The norm is not what is said, not even what is intended. The norm for preaching is what is *heard*. The ability of the preacher to enter into relationship is primary. Some preachers exist in an aura of sensitivity. They receive a constant flow of communication from the congregation. They anticipate what people hear. The perceptive preacher forms images and then corrects those images on the basis of feedback from the congregation.

We can never train able preachers if we neglect formation of relationships. Preachers must have the ability to feel with, the skill to establish common consciousness, and the knack to form a partnership with the congregation. This is the context in which the Word is spoken *and heard.*

The small church provides a setting in which the preacher and the congregation can be in close relationship. In intimate groups people are more willing to share openly.

The Responsive Congregation

The new denominational liturgies encourage participation by the congregation. Following the sermon, there is a major section in many of these liturgies for response. Liturgies for weddings and funerals include acts of response. Rubrics clearly indicate that the members of the congregation are invited to speak and take active roles in the services. Modern liturgies are a return to the worship of the early church, where members of the congregation actively participated.

The small church is the responsive congregation. Individuals don't get lost in the crowd. Each person is known, and any response is anticipated and understood. Responses are often called forth.

Provision for response is more specific than in the large

church. Possible responses are considered with more precision. A situation is created where response is not only possible but encouraged as well. In the small church, members feel responsible for responding.

In the last decade, several liturgical acts have been introduced into worship that call forth response. A period prior to prayer when the congregation can respond with joys and concerns is one such liturgical action. Each congregation has its own unique personality. Some churches resist prayer responses regardless of form or frequency. Many congregations have embraced this new style of praying with enthusiasm.

There is a direct correlation between size and willingness of a congregation to respond. Large churches have difficulty getting prayer responses from members of the congregation. Even if there are several responses, those responses represent participation by a small percentage of the people. In many large churches, the people feel little responsibility for volunteering concerns for prayer. Probably they do not know the people or share in the concerns named in the prayers.

The small church is a very different situation. Here, people know the other people and their concerns well. The prayers represent their own concerns. Participation involves a high percentage of the members of the church. People are more likely to share joys and concerns and to join in the prayers.

Decision Making in the Small Church

Members of small churches are accustomed to participating in decision making. Decision making is more informal than in large churches, but it represents a deeper sense of investment in the church. Agreement is reached at a board meeting, or decisions are made by the group that "comes to church." Often these occasions for decision making in the small church follow morning worship. The meeting is a continuation of worship, and everyone is likely to be involved.

There has been a drift toward modeling church decision making after secular decision making. The board room of the corporation has become the model. Churches want to be "businesslike." The result is that church decisions are made outside the worship context. There is little more awareness of the presence and will of God in church voting than there is in the business board room. Once churches seriously prayed about important decisions. Members sought to know the will of God about a matter before they voted on it. A consensus of the Spirit was reached in such a prayerful church meeting.

The model provided here—preaching in the responsive congregation—is an attempt to provide congregational involvement in both individual and corporate decision making and to return church decision making to the worship context.

How Decisions Are Made

Making decisions is a complex procedure. Few people know how they make decisions or what influences the decision making process. It is to the advantage of our commercial system to keep it that way. Sales people understand this. They have theory and practice well designed to help them influence decision making. Merchandising, as it is called, is predicated on selling what the supplier wants to sell, not on what the customer wants to buy. That is not quite correct. Merchandising intends to convince the customer that he or she wants to buy what the supplier has to sell.

Group decisions are equally influenced. A major industry in this country is the business of packaging political candidates so that the populace will elect them. Charitable causes are similarly merchandised, as are television evangelists and denominational programs. The church is deeply involved in the business of shaping decisions.

The church should be clear about its ethics. Both means and ends must be examined. Good results are not enough. People needs to be equipped to participate in making judgments. The process of making decisions should be open and honest. The motivated sequence, as presented in chapter 3, is often modified and shaped into a sales methodology. The motivated sequence and the pattern of reflective thinking may be used in helping church people raise questions, gather information, and choose between alternatives. As people understand the techniques, they can be full participants in decision making. In the small church, people need to trust the method as well as the people who share in reaching decisions. If this part of the work of the church is not discovered to be trustworthy, members of the congregation will be hesitant to take other members into the confidence of their personal decisions.

We turn now to a series of models for preaching. Each is

designed to encourage congregational participation, and each includes decision making.

The Evangelistic Model

Protestant preaching on the American frontier was designed to elicit a response. Sometimes described as "preaching for a verdict," this kind of preaching called for a decision at the conclusion of the sermon. The altar call, rather than the sermon, was the climax of the service. A powerful style of preaching—Protestant revivalistic preaching—ended with a dramatic call for action.

In many churches, preaching for personal decision is still the staple. The historic model of revivalism is followed. Prospects for conversion are generated by the church. These prospects come to hear the gospel proclaimed. This gospel includes repentance, confession, and forgiveness. The sermon calls for personal decision, and some form of response is encouraged. Generally this involves movement of penitents to the front of the sanctuary, personal prayer, and public witness to God's forgiveness. Persons who respond to the revivalistic sermon are nurtured, supported, and cared for as a part of the life of the church.

Depending on the tradition, other responses may be sought—renewal, sanctification, the gift of the Spirit, or other demonstrations of God's continuing activity in people's lives. Some churches provide healing services modeled after this style.

Many churches, especially small churches, have been unable to maintain this style of preaching for personal decision. As mentioned in chapter 1, the situation has changed. The church does not generate many prospects for conversion, and it seems inappropriate to neglect the nurture of loyal members in favor of an occasional visitor. In other churches there has been a cultural or theological shift so that newer evangelistic forms are used. Some churches perceive that revivalistic methods themselves have shifted so that they are no longer fit expressions of the life and beliefs of the church. These churches see modern revivalistic methods as manipulative, so the responses sought are not invited but coerced. They raise the same ethical questions about decision making in the revival setting that was raised earlier in this chapter about advertising.

Many small congregations are caught in this crunch. Whatever the reason, the altar call for personal decision following the sermon is no longer a norm for their worship. Sometimes this produces a kind of curtailed sermon in which the minister preaches in the old way, but stops short of the call for decision. Such a sermon ends with a summary or conclusion, not with a call for action.

Other churches modify and broaden the altar call. They call for responses that fit the congregation. An occasional call for recommitment is of this sort. A call for a specific response, such as the joining of a covenant group or participation in a Lenten emphasis, may be of this kind. Special services, as at the conclusion of a confirmation class, may include an altar call for personal decision. To call the people to pray for a special cause, or to call them to kneel at the Lord's Table for Holy Communion, may be other expressions of a modified altar call.

In the small church where participatory preaching is an option, the congregation may be invited to join in a preaching event in which responses are elicited throughout the sermon. People participate all along the way as well as at the end. In this model, the congregation participates in defining the occasion, in determining the nature of the decision to be made, in giving the sermon biblical grounding, in issuing the call to decision, and in making the final decision. There is less danger of unethical manipulation when the congregation participates fully in this way. Uncertainty is clarified. Alternate responses are suggested. The people and the minister together shape the whole event.

The story of Nicodemus is often used in revivalistic preaching. In the participatory model, the preacher guides the people through a retelling of the presenting story found in the third chapter of John. An overlay of a second, participating story follows or accompanies the Nicodemus story. This second story follows the same plot, but it causes Nicodemus to reflect modern anxieties and uncertainties. Jesus' responses answer our modern concerns. The third chapter of John includes a summary of the gospel for many people. A *kerygma*, or gospel, should provide theological grounding for the presenting and participating stories. A preacher making preparation for this sermon needs to exegete John's story with care. A sequence of questions might be developed as follows.

1. What kind of person was Nicodemus?
2. Why did he come at night?
3. What does he want?
4. What kind of response is Jesus asking for from Nicodemus?
5. What does "to be born again" mean?
6. What would that mean in our lives?
7. How do you know when the Spirit moves among us?

The minister or someone in the congregation comes to the realization that Nicodemus is looking for something he can do. Jesus points to something completely beyond what we can do. It is done only by God out of God's great love for us. The minister and the congregation outline the meaning of the new birth and ways of seeking it. Together the people issue an invitation. Then members of the congregation respond to their own invitation.

Other kinds of personal decisions may be sought using this model.

The Social Issues Model

Just as some churches have nostalgia for frontier revivalistic religion, so also others long for the social activism of the 1960s. Both evangelistic and social issues models illustrate important aspects of the gospel. Both involve personal and group decisions. They ask questions and seek answers: "What is the problem?" "What can I (we) do about it?"

Social issues involve personal decisions. They also demand group decisions. It is the occasions when the group must make a choice that cause greatest difficulty. Personal choices, such as signing a petition or joining a march, are clear-cut. Often, however, the power of the institution as a force in the larger community is needed to deal with a systemic problem. Then, the petition needs to be identified as one being circulated by the church, and the march needs to be identified as sponsored by the local church.

Local church programs are designed and presented to the congregation for implementation. Money from the church treasury is voted to support some effort. In these cases, the church acts as church and not as a collection of individuals.

How does the church make such corporate decisions? I suggest a participatory sermon as an appropriate and fair means of enabling group decisions.

Though participatory preaching will not be used to reach decisions about social issues every Sunday, the alert congregation will find many occasions when this methodology is useful.

The small church may have overlooked or underestimated its influence. We imagine that groups must be large if they are to have influence. In fact, many of the influential groups of our time are quite small. Compared with other denominations, Mennonites are very small; yet, their influence has been large concerning peace issues. I was pastor of a small church where a minor committee asked the church board to petition the city council to desegregate the community swimming pool. The church board agreed, although they said, "Nothing much will happen because we're not one of the big churches in town." They were surprised when the city council listened courteously, argued intently, and at the next meeting voted in favor of "the church resolution."

Walter Brueggemann's basic thesis in *The Prophetic Imagination* is, "The task of prophetic ministry is to nurture, nourish, and evoke a consciousness and perception alternative to the consciousness and perception of the dominant culture around us."[1]

This prophetic imagination provides a useful method in dealing with many biblical passages and their implications for the church. My use of this method in preaching hinges on three questions: (1) How do most people in our culture feel and think about this issue? (2) Is there a different way Christians should feel and think about this issue? (3) What are the implications?

Just asking these questions sparks insightful dialogue in congregations. The questions help a local church to discuss its involvement in the dominant culture and to detail how this congregation can develop its own consciousness and perspective. Brueggemann's idea of "offering an alternative perception of reality and in letting people see their own history in the light of God's freedom and his will for justice"[2] works best when the people have participated in the offering of the alternatives themselves.

Following Brueggemann's model, the small church examines how Moses represents a radical challenge to the social structures of Pharaoh's Egypt. They ask whether "royal consciousness" characterizes our own cultural situation, and what alternate consciousness the church will represent. Action concerning a local expression of "royal consciousness" completes the sermon.

Who raises these social issues? Ministers usually assume that raising such issues is part of the prophetic ministry of the clergy, and they are often right. Occasionally, however, the denomination will raise social issues. Pastoral letters from the bishops of the Roman Catholic Church in the United States have raised questions concerning our economic system and our nation's recourse to nuclear deterrence. The bishops of The United Methodist Church recently issued a pastoral letter "In Defense of Creation." Copies of the letter and a supporting book were provided to congregations of that church.[3] It was an occasion for discussion, debate, and decision. In some congregations, public meetings were convened, and people were encouraged to discuss issues involved in the letter. Committees were named to do additional research and to report back to the congregation. The pastoral letter became an occasion for the local church to enter into decision making.

The prophetic ministry of the church belongs to the whole church. The people need to be deeply involved in raising the issues, in discussing various avenues of response, and in making decisions. Clergy or denominational boards or agencies cannot assume responsibility that finally belongs to members of the church. We need to find ways of restoring this ministry to the people. Of course, the people can use all the resources denominations provide.

When a participatory preaching model is used, people need to be prepared to participate in depth and equipped to make informed and Christian decisions. The model becomes a valuable form of Christian education.

As the congregation wrestles with the issue in its public meeting, members should be free to interrupt the talk and pause for reflection and prayer. Anyone in the group is free to ask for such a moment, but the preacher should be particularly sensitive to the need for recourse to prayer.

The role of the preacher changes in this kind of preaching from one who reaches unilateral decisions and announces them to the people to one who helps the church raise and deal with issues. The preacher in this role is a member of the group who is seeking to understand a difficult situation and to find Christian ways of dealing with it. This is a threatening and unfamiliar role for some clergy. However, it develops a model for decision making and the managing of conflict that can serve clergy well in many settings. Some members of the congregation may also be threatened by the expectation of decision making in a worship service. Social issues often are confused and complicated by mixed motives. People may be uncomfortable sorting out their motives in public. The community must be very sensitive to these ambivalent feelings and not push people beyond where they want to go. As we shall see, there are ways of referral and of stopping short of final decision. However, occasionally the intimate community can work through the decision making process and arrive at conclusions that are highly satisfying. They have moved beyond uncertainty and discomfort to arrive at decisions that represent Christian consensus. In addition, the congregation may feel that they have participated in a kind of New Testament experience in which the Holy Spirit guides the church into truth. Uneasiness should not hinder the church from taking its prophetic role.

A Model for Doctrinal Issues

There is a double bind in doctrinal sermons. Most churches are uneasy about doctrinal issues. They want to be pluralistic and welcome persons of any faith background. They are hesitant to give anyone authority in these matters. Yet, a common complaint is, "We don't know what we believe!" "What does the church stand for?" The creeds we recite sound general and out of touch with modern concerns. Doctrinal sermons, if preached at all in the modern church, attempt to be uncontroversial.

I remember a seminary professor who taught historical theology. Each class session, I was amazed how those old issues always were nudged into contemporary conflict under his hand. I'd like a return to doctrinal preaching, but not ossified, textbook preaching. The historic issues still matter. The *practice* of the church, rather than its lip service, reveals what we believe about doctrine. It's difficult to convince me that prayer is central to a church that has virtually eliminated it from worship. Infrequent communion says more than articles of religion about how a church values the sacaments.

When the lessons include I Corinthians 11:23-26, the sermon in the small church can formulate such questions for discussion as:

1. Can a modern person believe in sacraments? (Exegete I Cor. 11:27-32 with care!)
2. What does "This is my body" mean?
3. What are the results of "proclaiming the death of the Lord"?
4. How often shall we celebrate the Lord's Supper?
5. How can our celebration reflect Paul's understanding of the Lord's Supper?

Preparation for dealing with doctrinal issues should send some members of the congregation back to biblical and historical sources. Others might examine contemporary implications. Consideration of doctrinal issues gives everyone a sense of standing within an ecclesial tradition and develops sensitivity to God's working within the church.

Life Situation Model

I'm not concerned with sermons on "How to Stop Worrying" or "How to Get More Out Of Life." Such preaching seldom involves the congregation in making hard choices. People join in preaching more actively if there is a controversial decision to be made. Everyone quietly agrees that we should worry less and pray more. Responses become more vigorous in sermons that deal with divorce, inclusive language, and caring for the aging. We need persons who have first hand experience with the issues. They should have a chance to share their experiences, and they may be asked in advance to do so. Biblical resources help to get the issue in perspective. What the church has said about this issue at different times can also be revealing. Finally we must turn to discovery of a distinctively Christian way of dealing with this issue today. As members of the congregation struggle and listen to hear God's will for a life issue, they learn to do theology—to look for God's activity in the common experiences of daily life.

Reader: "After washing their feet and taking his garments again, he sat down. 'Do you understand what I have done for you?' " (John 13:12 NEB).

Preacher: We always think we understand when a thing is happening, but remembering it later, we realize much went over our heads.

Response: The disciples thought Jesus was just doing a job that needed to be done.

Response: I remember Jane taking care of her mother. That was a chore none of the other kids wanted to do.

Response: Yes, and it wasn't just once. Her mother had to be taken care of all the time. She washed her mother's feet "and head and hands" every day.

Response: We knew it had to be done, but we didn't know what a servant ministry it was until we remembered later.

Preacher: How do we restore such a servant ministry to the church?

The Biblical Model

Properly speaking, there is not a biblical model. All preaching should be biblical. To study the Bible for its own sake is to risk turning a means into an end. That is not to say that there is no value in studying a book, a kind of biblical literature, or a passage. Working through a book of the Bible may have excellent educational value, but it is not necessarily good preaching. A sermon is an occasion to hear the Word. It is not primarily an occasion to learn about the written words of the Bible. There must be another agenda, an agenda in which the Holy Spirit inspires people so that the inspired words of the Bible may speak again.

A second problem with the biblical model presented in this chapter is that it seldom generates decision making. Therefore, the biblical model as a way of stimulating response from the congregation will generally be used in connection with the determination of hermeneutical method. Gradually, the small church develops a method of Bible study. An occasional participatory sermon that examines the issues of Bible use and tries to make judgments as to how the Bible is to be used can be helpful.

Karl Barth deals with the Word of God in three categories.[4] First is the revealed word. This is the starting point for Barthian theology—God's act in Jesus Christ. Second is the written Word. Placing the Bible in this secondary relationship to the revealed Word keeps it in perspective. Third is what Barth often calls the preached Word, an active and inspiring Word proclaimed in the church. A congregation needs to learn to listen for this Word and to be guided by it in decision making.

There are conflicts in accounts of events. Most are unimportant for preaching, but some have significant implications for the modern congregation. Matthew and Mark have very similar accounts of events in the life of Jesus, but occasionally they differ. These conflicts are significant because they represent an intentional difference in interpretation. Congregations can investigate these differences and decide which version of the account will guide their own interpretation.

Finally, some passages present problems just because they address difficult issues that remain controversial in the modern church. Paul's views of the role of women is such an issue that presses the modern church to rethink roles in the church. What authority does Paul's opinion on this matter have?

What Is the Sermon Sequence?

There are many ways to shape a sermon leading to decision making. Form ought to follow function. The shape, as well as the content, of the sermon should help people make up their minds. In general, decision making begins with an issue or question and moves toward a solution. Care is taken to keep this sequence from being simplistic. Congregational participation usually provides enough complication for what the preacher thought was a simple issue.

Begin by Raising Existential Questions

Occasionally one of the scripture lessons asks the question. Usually not. Lectionary lessons stress conclusions rather than opening questions. It is worthwhile to look behind the lesson to ask what question it is answering. Then, ask that contextual question with contemporary force. Sometimes the lesson asks a question. Still, it must be searched to find contemporary implications.

The existential question may come from our own lives.[5] A person speaking out of his or her own experience asks the question with special impact. The question may be raised with feeling in drama or literature, especially if some of the people have seen or read it recently. Drama and literature portray our human predicament forcefully. A narrative, biblical or contemporary, establishes the problem better than propositional speech.

Sometimes we ask the wrong questions. Barth reminded us of how our human perspective warps all our questions. A gospel corrective may need to be applied, but that is a matter for discussion. The human perspective is finally the only one we have.

Whether the issues are raised by the lesson, by the preacher, by the denomination, or by a committee, the congregation needs to feel that they are authentic questions. The people need to claim the questions as their very own. Some time should be spent testing to determine that the issue is a real one for these people today.

Theological Answers

Finding theological answers is no easier than asking existential questions. Analysis of the question is part of the theological answer. Analysis is also necessary for any proposed answers. There is an active role for the people as they do such analysis. Resources and expert opinion need to be brought to the sermon, but this is not the exclusive role of the preacher, as in conventional preaching. Inductive cases, personal testimony, or reading reports may be assigned to members of the congregation. Resource persons may be arranged for any given sermon—a mortician when the subject is the American way of death, shut-ins when aging is the issue, a lawyer when divorce is discussed, and youth when drug use among young people is the concern. The preacher has outlined a sequence and knows what the special resources are. The preacher summarizes, asks for input from a source, compares responses, asks additional questions, and makes comments—in short, keeps the sequence on track toward a major discovery of the gospel.

Scripture lessons will play a definitive role in this process. Sometimes they supply the narrative vehicle. Often the lectionary lessons express and summarize an important biblical insight. Such insight can't be experienced as a word for our situation until the situation is relived.

Once the congregation lives its way into the existential problem, it is ready for alternative answers. The special treasury of the church is its theological perspective. Members learn, as they use this methodology, to look at problems from a gospel perspective (or with prophetic imagination). The preacher or another member of the congregation suddenly experiences an "aha" that pulls question and answer together in a creative new arrangement. This discovery breaks open all kinds of new implications for the members of the community.

End by Making Decisions

An action step completes this kind of preaching. The decision is possible because of what happened during the sermon. The members of the group participated in formulating the question and in seeking theological answers. Now they are ready for action. The decision to be made may be a personal one. The preacher issues an invitation to personal decision, and members of the congregation may respond in some agreed on manner. Or a group decision is required, and the whole congregation makes a corporate choice.

A combination of personal and group decision may be made. Decisions that affect the mission of the church are of this type. Sometimes decisions are a combination of decision making and abatement of decision. This occurs when the group is not yet ready to decide. The issue may be assigned to committee for further work or to a standing committee of the church for final decision and implementation. In the case of a congregational decision about a pastoral letter from the bishops of the church, the local church may decide to sponsor a complete study of the issue. They might decide to issue a press release or draw up a petition. Members may lobby the city council to make this a nuclear free town. Action may be taken to join a peace organization. The church might object to the letter and make its negative witness to the bishops. Another option is to make this an open issue and hold a time for prayer in which each member of the congregation makes his or her own personal decision.

This congregation is not only responsive, but it is also growing toward maturity. Members are learning to handle scripture and make private and group decisions. They learn in the process how to handle conflict, and they lose much of their nervousness about it. All issues that matter have conflict as a central component. Gradually they will learn that the church is the right place for conflict. The church isn't fragile. It doesn't have to be protected from difference of opinion. If the church is sheltered from the conflict in our society, it will be unable to know the nature of the questions and will have no basis for which to supply answers.

The intimate group is the right size for the use of this method. It is also best equipped to support response and to make decisions.

The local congregation is being encouraged to be more responsive. Liturgical actions provide means of participation. A sermonic method that makes it possible to discuss issues and reach decisions is needed. The church will respond with vigor when members are convinced that the issues to be decided are important ones and that their response matters.

6

Worship and Preaching in the Small Church

After the people have gathered, the traditional call to worship is the ringing of the church bell. As the note of the bell dies, Wanda moves to the piano, and we sing a hymn. During the singing, Steve and Doris set the table. They spread a white linen cloth over the table that always stands at the front of our church, and they light a candle.[1]

As the hymn ends, Uncle John moves forward and kneels so that he faces the congregation across the table. He prays, and we all join in the praying, for it is the prayer we have all learned from him.

> Almighty God, unto whom all hearts are open, all desires known, and from whom no secrets are hid; Cleanse the thoughts of our hearts by the inspiration of thy Holy Spirit, that we may perfectly love thee, and worthily magnify thy holy name; through Christ our Lord. *Amen.*[2]

Joyce sings a *hallel* (a psalm of praise).[3] We all join in singing the doxology at the end.

> Praise the Lord, all God's servants.
> Praise the name of the Lord.
> Blessed be the God of Israel;
> The One who reigns forevermore.
> From the rising to the setting
>   of the sun,
> God's name be praised.

> High above all nations honored,
> There is none like the Lord our God!
>
> Come to worship all God's children.
> Bow before the Lord our God!
> Gather 'round God's Supper Table.
> Praise the Lord for God is here!
> Praise the Lo'rd, the Creator.
> God Incarnate, Jesus Christ.
> Praise the Spirit who is with us
> Calling us to be the Church.

Readers rise in the congregation and read the lessons, including one of the accounts of the Lord's Supper.

The preacher stands among the members of the congregation and asks, "What is the setting of this story?"

The people talk about the place and the feeling of the place, about the time and a sense of the times.

"Who are the characters?" the preacher asks.

"Mostly it's about Jesus," someone responds.

"Tell us about him."

Members talk about Jesus in the upper room, how he has come to this hour, who he is, and what he is about.

The preacher asks about the other characters.

"Can we describe the disciples and how they feel?"

Then the sermon turns to the problem that hangs in the air. They have already described the disciples' fear. They connect them up with an oppressed people. This little group is away from home and has a sense of separation. Most important, death has a cold grip on them.

The preacher turns and walks to the pulpit. "The Passover meal has caused the disciples to relive a time when they were slaves, when God brought them out of Egypt. All their worst fears were being realized. Wasn't

Jesus talking about death when he added that surprising ending to the meal, 'This is my body . . . this is my blood poured out'? God had brought them forth from slavery, but could God bring them forth from death? This is a meal that recognizes the reality of sin and death. It is also a meal that celebrates the presence of the *resurrected Lord*. It is a meal that gathers us around a table that anticipates a messianic banquet. The hope of that future banquet opens us to the presence of Jesus with us today. As we share in this meal, our sin and death are overcome. New life is given to us."

Alice and George bring the bread and wine and place them on the table. A woven basket is circulated through the congregation, receiving alms.

The prayers follow. Some members of the community go forward and kneel for prayer at the altar railing. First are the prayers of the people. We speak our joys and concerns, and the preacher gathers the prayer into one liturgical offering. Prayers of confession follow. These prayers are mostly silent, although occasionally someone will speak a confession for the whole community. The preacher pronounces absolution. A full eucharistic prayer is prayed by the preacher: "I greet you in the name of the Lord."

The people respond with their own greetings.

The preacher continues, "Let us give thanks to God."

Several people offer a sentence or two of thanksgiving. The Peace may be passed at this point. People move slowly and caringly from person to person saying, "The peace of God is with you."

Then we sing the Sanctus.[5]

The preacher retells the story of the Lord's Supper as the central focus of the prayer. There are certain familiar phrases that have passed down through the tradition, such as: "On the night in which he was betrayed" and "Do this in remembrance of me."

The prayer is not read from a worship book or from the Bible. It is told like a story, and the people may be invited to tell this central story of the faith when it has not been the subject of the sermon. The minister is careful to supply what is called the remembrance. It is more than recalling. This remembrance recognizes the real presence of Jesus Christ and helps the people experience again the death and resurrection of the Lord. The minister also includes in the prayer an invocation of the Holy Spirit, asking that the Spirit will cause this bread and wine to become for us the body and blood of Jesus Christ. The prayer ends with praise and then everyone joins in the Lord's Prayer.[6]

We all gather around the table following the prayer and greet one another across the table. We pass the bread and the chalice from hand to hand, each of us addressing one another by name and saying, "The body of Jesus Christ . . . the cup of the new covenant." When everyone has received the bread and wine, we sing a hymn while standing around the table. It is a hymn to which we all know the words. If there is any doubt about our knowing the lyrics, a member of the congregation lines out the hymn as we sing.

The good words are said as we stand holding hands around the table. "Go forth in peace remembering that the blessings of this community and the presence of God go with you. Amen."[7]

Every small church has its own distinctive personality and should develop its own worship patterns within the tradition of the Christian movement and the denomination to which it belongs. The service above reflects one such community.

We do need models for worship that take size into consideration. The communication situation that shapes the sermon in the small church—such as intimacy, shared story, flexibility—should also shape the worship experience.

Acts of worship have been mentioned with regularity in this discussion. It should be clear by now how closely related preaching and worship are in the small congregation. Preaching and worship are one thing rather than two. The participatory model for preaching works well in the small membership church because it links with acts of worship in which people share.

The Gathering

The way people gather for worship signals what is to follow. The setting—time and place—puts certain parameters around the service. The meeting, the recognition, and the first exchanges of the people set the direction for the whole worship experience. Many kinds of symbolic communication set the tone: Do we stand awkwardly on the front steps? Do we rock the babies and talk while our eyes follow the children? Are there classes that set the stage for worship? Do we warm our fingers around coffee cups? Do the families split into age and gender groups as they arrive or blend in an intergenerational gathering? Often congregations are unsure of how to gather for worship.

Jim felt uneasy about the beginning of the worship service. People visited, talking aloud during the piano prelude. Sometimes it was difficult to get their attention in order to begin the first hymn.

Personal prayer, quiet time, and appreciation of the music were appropriate ways to begin worship, in Jim's mind. It didn't take long for him to realize that this small congregation had a very different image of the proper start for the service. For them, friendly visitation was the appropriate activity when they came together before the church service.

Finally, Jim and several members of the church sat down and discussed the matter. They decided that they were both right. Community formation was important. It was also important to prepare in prayer for the service. There needed to be clear signals that were understood and agreed upon by the community to help them prepare for worship.

They decided that welcoming, visiting, and friendly exchanges should come first. It was natural in the small group to talk during the activities of gathering, preparing the sanctuary, and getting ready to worship. They also decided to be intentional during this period to welcome anyone new in the community.

How were they all to know when to turn from friendly visitation to prayer and personal preparation for worship? The beginning of the piano prelude might signal this change, but members of the congregation had ignored this in the past. The lighting of the candles might indicate that the period of prayer had begun. The preacher might go forward, kneel, and pray silently as a model for other members of the congregation. The ringing of the bell could be heard distinctly inside the building, and that would be clear communication of the beginning of the prayer time. The bell, they decided, would be the signal for moving from friendly visitation to quiet prayer.

There are many subtle ways to communicate a change or transition from one activity to another. These signals should be as closely connected to the desired results as possible, and the community needs to agree on their use.

Singing

Singing has always been a part of Christian worship. Almost every part of the worship service has been sung at some time in the tradition. Singing adds heightened expression, communal sharing, and inspiration. Yet, no part of worship is more problematic than singing in many small membership churches. Lack of instrumental accompaniment, strong leading voices, and sometimes lack of imagination will stymie singing.

"Let's ask the Williamson girls to sing a special number for us at church some Sunday."

"I didn't know they could sing."

"Of course they do—that is, they sing at home all the time. I understand they both sing in the choir at school. Caroline even plays the guitar."

It began that way. The Williamson girls, Caroline and Cindy, agreed to sing a duet during worship. That became a regular occurrence. When there was difficulty with accompaniment, Caroline began playing her guitar. One Sunday, they invited the congregation to sing along on the chorus. Soon they were the regular song leaders for the congregation. They recruited a few other singers, and in a short time the church had a youth choir that provided leadership for congregational singing and service music. The whole service of worship was renewed.

"Did you know that Charlie is taking piano lessons?"

That inquiry about a junior high member of the congregation led to a special arrangement in which Charlie and his piano teacher took responsibility for training and providing piano accompaniment for the church's singing.

A small congregation doesn't have to have accompaniment for singing, but it helps. Instruments other than the piano or the organ may be utilized. Sometimes recorded accompaniment may be used. Provision for good music leadership should be a priority for the church—and it need not be beyond the resources of the smallest church.

Music supports other acts of worship—calls to worship, calls to prayer, responses to scripture, and the like. The congregation can provide this service music by singing verses of hymns or by using simple service music. It need not be changed often and can become a valued and distinctive part of the worship of a particular level church.

Praying

Sometimes choirs take over singing, and ministers take over praying. Both should be returned to the congregation. In the last decade, the raising of joys and concerns in preparation for prayer has become common practice. Small membership churches often ask members of the congregation to pray, or they may encourage a kind of prayer that utilizes a series of sentence prayers or prayer responses by the people.

Concern for one another in a small congregation is personal and pressing. Spontaneous prayer often grows out of the immediate need of someone in the community. "Ask the church to pray for me." "Let's remember to pray for Aunt Fern, who is in the hospital at Steeleville."

Responsorial prayer is being used more. A member of the congregation prays, "for Judy, who has just gone off to college, let us pray to the Lord." The congregation responds, "Lord, hear our prayer." "That the rain may stop so that we can get in the fields, let us pray to the Lord." "Lord, hear our prayer."

Joining hands, gathering around the altar, and singing before and after prayer all fit action to prayer. Prayer also supports other acts of worship. The offertory prayer and the prayer of illumination before the scripture reading both prepare the people for a specific act of worship. Members of the congregation will sometimes make the praying of such prayers their responsibility. Silent prayer, versicles, and standard prayers, such as the Lord's Prayer, all emphasize the participation of the congregation.

Blessing and healing are significant parts of biblical praying. The intimate community can best reclaim these prayers in contemporary forms. Blessings indicate that this church is participating in and carrying forward the will of God. Churches dedicate buildings, organs, and homes. The small community can dedicate leaders and teachers. It can send people forth with blessings. The blessings are closely tied to the good intention of this community. The church prays for God's good will to accompany this person or to protect this building. This is supported and given additional meaning by the good will of the community itself.

Congregation involvement may be clearer in the use of prayers for healing. The small congregation matches its prayers for healing with acts showing concern and ministry. God's good will is invoked, and the members of the church visit the ill, bring food, care for the family, and contribute to the needs of the one who is sick. Prayers for healing and blessing are much more closely bound to community action in the small church and contain less danger of sliding into empty ritual or magical incantation.

Prayers supported by community action are not limited to the church building in small congregations. The whole congregation may move to another place, as when they go to the home of a sick person for prayer.

The Lord's Supper

In some denominations small membership churches have been denied the sacraments because of lack of ordained clergy. Even when this has been rectified, it takes time and education for the people to desire more frequent celebration of the sacraments. However, in the last decade there has been a dramatic increase in the appreciation of and demand for more frequent communion. Protestant denominations—such as the Disciples—and Roman Catholics, who practice celebration of the eucharist every Sunday, refute the old fear that frequent celebration of communion causes the rite to lose its meaning.

The small membership church provides a setting like that of early Christian use—the house church. Often the whole church can gather at one time around the table. Prayers, songs, and blessings may occur as the congregation receives bread and wine. Third century liturgies incorporated pastoral concerns into this part of the service, praying for the sick, remembering the dead, and blessing the faithful. Such acts may be restored to the Lord's Supper when they are the natural pastoral concerns of the congregation.

The eucharistic prayer, or prayer of consecration, may be in the language of the people. It does not have to be read word-for-word from the book. It is not a rambling pastoral prayer. It does need to include the general outline of the narrative of the upper room, the remembrance, the invocation, and the doxology. These portions of the prayer, and all the prayers of the service, may be prayed as in the early Christian church—as best as the presider can.

A service that includes group singing, face-to-face communication, participatory preaching, and that concludes by moving around a table is a family service. The small membership church is best equipped to celebrate this type of service.

Special Occasions

Baptisms, weddings, funerals, renewal of vows, ordination, confirmation—the large church calendar is filled with these activities. They often occur outside the gathered worship services of the congregation. When they are included in gathered worship, they are often rushed or treated as incidental.

In the small congregation, these are momentous events that occur infrequently and that command the attention of the whole church. Too often, the small membership church has followed the pattern set by the large church and has relegated these special events to private services. They are welcome in the Sunday morning service because everyone is interested in these special events, and everyone wants to participate. The new liturgies say that baptism means being welcomed into the family of God. In the small congregation, that is what happens. There are few baptisms, weddings, or confirmations in the small membership church. Each event offers an occasion to emphasize for the whole congregation a special facet of the gospel.

Why are funerals or memorial services so seldom incorporated into Sunday morning worship services? In many places, funerals are not even held in the church building. Death may not occur so that it is possible for the funeral to be held as part of the regular Sunday service, but a memorial service could be part of that service. If the funeral is held on a weekday, still the service should be in the church sanctuary and look like Sunday morning worship. "The Christian funeral is as much an act of corporate worship as any other worship activity, and the heart of the proclamation at a Christian funeral, as at any other Christian service, is the gospel message of death and resurrection."[8]

The funeral service may include hymn singing; use of congregational prayers; a participatory eulogy; and a special act of the passing of the peace, which gives members of the community a chance to speak to one another, to pray for one another, and to share their intimate hopes and fears. It may not occur on Sunday morning, but in any case it will be an important event if it is the funeral of a participant in a small congregation. It should be a time when the congregation can gather in the sanctuary to participate in the remembering of the dead and the worship of God.

Levels of Participation

Group participation is most important. Singing, responsive reading, passing of the peace, and receiving the Lord's Supper all enable the congregational family to do things together.

The small membership church should also be intentional about shared leadership. Praying, reading scripture, special music, ushering, and serving the congregation combine service and recognition and should be shared through the congregation. This leadership should be intergenerational, include both men and women, and break across social, racial, and cultural boundaries.

Sharing of leadership builds a reservoir of resources. Often the small membership church believes that it lacks resources. If someone will be intentional about expanding these resources and keeping record of their use, the church will be amazed at what and who is available. Who can take pictures and make the photographs public? Who can make banners? What instruments are available for the music of the church? Is there a storyteller in the community? Who will bake the bread? Who will rehearse the reading? Train the acolytes? Help serve communion? Provide transportation? Make the coffee?

Helen has a friend who is willing to come occasionally to provide special music. Joe uses a copier at work and can copy bulletins. The Bible study class can do a choral reading of the psalm. There are more resources than we thought. This participation enriches the worship and provides meaningful investment by more people in the service.

The Worship of the People

Worship is generally the focusing activity in the life of the small membership church. All the church's programming emanates from this center. Therefore, the worship service needs to be connected to the lives, concerns, and needs of the congregation. The worship service should reflect denominational practice, but prior to this it should mirror the life of this particular people. Our most imaginative leaders import styles of worship from other churches—usually large churches. Imagination and creativity directed toward discovering the needs and resources of this local community are much more productive. Sunday worship and preaching need to speak to the people gathered, develop and express their faith, allow them to participate, and reflect who they are and who God wants them to become.

N O T E S

Introduction

1. Lyle E. Schaller, "United Methodist Churches: Fewer but Tougher?" *Circuit Rider* (April 1987):13.

1. Challenges to Preaching in a Small Congregation

1. Reuel L. Howe, *Partners in Preaching* (New York: The Seabury Press, 1967), summarized from chapter 4.
2. Dietrich Bonhoeffer, *Life Together* (New York: Harper & Row, 1976), pp. 8, 20.
3. William H. Willimon, *Sunday Dinner* (Nashville: The Upper Room, 1981).

2. Communication in the Small Congregation

1. Lyle E. Schaller, *The Small Church Is Different* (Nashville: Abingdon Press, 1982). In the preface, Schaller says, "The normal size for a Protestant congregation on the North American continent is one that has fewer than forty people at worship on the typical Sunday morning." On page 58 he says, "If the average attendance at the service is used to measure size, one half of all Protestant churches in the United States and Canada average fewer than seventy-five at worship."
2. Ibid., p. 19.
3. Carl S. Dudley, *Making the Small Church Effective* (Nashvile: Abingdon Press, 1978), p. 32. He goes on to say, "In a primary group, members are united by common interests, beliefs, tasks, and territory. . . . They have a solidarity, a feeling of belonging, nourished by experiences of intimacy and personal need. The primary group is a folk society in the midst of the urban culture.

When so many other contacts are temporary and impersonal, the primary group provides the atmosphere of an extended family.

Like the primary group, the small church develops and confirms the ideals of individuals in the context of its own character and strength. Like the primary family group, the small church offers intimacy and reassurance among those who can be trusted. Like the extended family, many small churches have a territorial identify with a particular place. . . . Like the family-clan, the church family often carries the food, rhythm, and culture of a particular ethnic, racial, or national group."

4. Schaller, *The Small Church Is Different*, pp. 133-34.
5. David R. Ray, *Small Churches Are the Right Size* (New York: The Pilgrim Press, 1982) Ray titles chapter 3 "Worship: The Family Reunion of the Body of Christ." He emphasizes participation, particularly in worship. There is little treatment of preaching.
6. William Willimon and Robert Wilson, *Preaching and Worship in the Small Church* (Nashville: Abingdon Press, 1980), p. 26. "A larger proportion of the members of a small congregation participate in the management of the church . . . persons in such congregations tend to have a strong sense of responsibility for, and ownership of, their church and its activities."
7. Schaller, *The Small Church Is Different*, p. 28. "The long-established Angle [small] church is usually built around a ministry of the laity." He lists three exceptions: (1) the new congregation, (2) black churches, and (3) congregations at the very conservative or very liberal end of the theological spectrum, or that is "independent."
8. Ray, *Small Churches Are the Right Size*, p. 43. "Knowledge of one another is crucial, because people behave differently and feel differently with people they know."
9. Ron Benefiel, "A Family in Mission," in Jon Johnston and Bill M. Sullivan, *The Smaller Church* (Kansas City: Beacon Hill Press, 1983), pp. 118-19.
10. Alan K. Waltz, "Organizational Structures for the Small Congregation," in *Small Churches Are Beautiful*, ed. Jackson W. Carroll (San Francisco: Harper & Row, 1977), p. 147. "The small congregation has no need or desire for a large and involved organizational structure. Many have established means for doing the necessary administrative work. They have few requirements in terms of the development, maintenance, and administration of facilities."

11. Schaller, *The Small Church Is Different*, pp. 30-31. "Most human beings tend to be more comfortable associating with people from the same age cohort. . . . By contrast, in many small churches, the dynamics of congregational life naturally tend to bring people together in repeated face-to-face contacts across generational lines.

   One of the most significant implications of this generalization is that the small rural church, along with the conservation movement, is one of the few places in American society in which the concept of intergenerational obligation is being perpetuated."

12. Ray, *Small Churches Are the Right Size*, p. 78. "When there are only a handful of births, baptisms, weddings, and deaths a year, the preacher can specifically and personally address the feelings that are part of them."

13. Edward W. Hassinger, et al., *A Comparison of Rural Churches and Ministers in Missouri Over a 35 Year Period.* Research Bulletin 999, University of Missouri-Columbia, College of Agriculture (Nov. 1973): 27. "It is hazardous to predict the future of the rural church, but its tenacity in a changing society suggests that another survey in a decade would find the bulk of the congregations operating at the same stand at about the same level of activity. They will continue to be essentially fellowship groups engaged in internal activities and a frustration for denominational executives."

14. Some authors list characteristics. See: Ray, *Small Churches Are the Right Size*, pp. 58-63; Schaller, *The Small Church Is Different*, pp. 28-41; L. Ray Sells and Ronald K. Crandall, *The Small Membership Church: Growing, Caring, Serving* (Nashville: Discipleship Resources, 1982), chapter 3.

15. See Jackson W. Carroll, *Small Churches Are Beautiful* (San Francisco: Harper & Row, 1977); Dudley, *Making the Small Church Effective* (Nashville: Abingdon Press 1978); Jon Johnston and Bill M. Sullivan, *The Smaller Church in a Super Church Era* (Kansas City: Beacon Hill Press, 1983); Paul O. Madsen, *The Small Church: Valid, Vital, Victorious* (Valley Forge, Penn.: Judson Press, 1975); Ray, *Small Churches are the Right Size*; Sells and Crandall, *The Small Membership Church: Growing, Caring, Serving.*

16. Willimon & Wilson, *Preaching and Worship in the Small Church*, p. 108.

17. Ray, *Small Churches Are the Right Size*, p. 57. He lists forty-five activities that might involve that many people in a congregation of fifty on a typical Sunday morning.

18. See the following examples: William J. Bausch, *Storytelling: Faith and Imagination* (Mystic, Conn.: Twenty-third Publications, 1984); George M. Bass, *The Song and the Story* (Lima, Ohio: C.S.S. Publishing Co., 1984); Richard A. Jensen, *Telling the Story* (Minneapolis: Augsburg Publishing House, 1980); Henry H. Mitchell, *The Recovery of Preaching* (San Francisco: Harper & Row, 1977); Edmund A. Steimle, Morris J. Niedenthal, and Charles L. Rice, *Preaching the Story* (Philadelphia: Fortress Press, 1980); Don M. Wardlaw, ed. *Preaching Biblically: Creating Sermons in the Shape of Scripture* (Philadelphia: The Westminster Press, 1983).

19. Jürgen Moltmann, *The Church in the Power of the Spirit* (New York: Harper & Row, 1977), p. 82.

3. Opening the Door to Participatory Preaching

1. Fred B. Craddock, *Preaching* (Nashville: Abingdon Press, 1985), p. 169.

2. Reuel L. Howe, *Partners in Preaching*, p. 43.

3. Ibid., p. 46.

4. Ibid., p. 47.

5. Ibid., p. 69.

6. O. C. Edwards, Jr., *The Living and Active Word* (New York: The Seabury Press, 1975), p. 63.

7. Halford E. Luccock, *In the Minister's Workshop* (New York: Nashville: Abingdon-Cokesbury, 1944). See pp. 56-57, where Luccock shows that Dewey's method is an improvement over older educational methods and a good model for "preaching to life situations."

8. Alan H. Monroe, *Principles and Types of Speech* (Chicago: Scott, Foresman and Co., 1949).

9. Eugene Lowry, *The Homiletical Plot* (Atlanta: John Knox Press, 1980), pp. 47-48.

10. R. E. C. Browne, *The Ministry of the Word* (Philadelphia: Fortress Press, 1976), p. 121.

11. Carl E. Braaten, *The Apostolic Imperative* (Minneapolis: Augsburg, 1985), p. 192.

4. Participatory Biblical Narrative Preaching

1. Sam Keen, *To a Dancing God* (New York: Harper & Row, 1970), pp. 8-13.

2. Gordon D. Fee, *New Testament Exegesis* (Philadelphia: The Westminster Press, 1983), p. 118.
3. H. R. Niebuhr, *The Meaning of Revelation* (New York: Macmillan, 1960), p. 93.
4. David Rhoads and Donald Michie, *Mark as Story* (Philadelphia: Fortress Press, 1982), p. xii.

5. Participatory Preaching and Decision Making

1. Walter Brueggemann, *The Prophetic Imagination* (Philadelphia: Fortress Press, 1978), p. 13.
2. Ibid., p. 110.
3. *In Defense of Creation*, The United Methodist Council of Bishops (Nashville: Graded Press, 1986).
4. Karl Barth, *Church Dogmatics*, vol. I, part I, (Edinburgh: T. & T. Clark, 1936), pp. 98-140.
5. See Paul Tillich, *Systematic Theology*, vol. I (Chicago: University of Chicago Press, 1951), pp. 59-66. Tillich's theological method is to ask existential questions and to give theological answers.

6. Worship and Preaching In the Small Church

1. Other liturgists add vesting, washing of hands, and other acts that reflect the particular liturgical season.
2. *The Book of Common Prayer* (New York: Seabury Press, 1953), p. 67.
3. *Hallel* means "praise." Hallel psalms are 113–118, and a few other psalms, such as 136 and 146–148. Joyce sings portions of these psalms to hymn tunes, making sure the tunes are joyous. She rewrites the words of the psalm into verses with the same meter as the tune. This one begins with Psalm 113 and adds an introit and doxology. The tune is "Hymn to Joy" often used for "Joyful, Joyful, We Adore Thee." She may accompany the singing with a guitar.
4. A collection of eucharistic prayers and an outline of the contents of eucharistic prayers is included in: *A Communion Service Book*, Supplemental Worship Resources #9 (Nashville: Abingdon Press, 1981).
5. We have learned various versions of:

   Holy, holy, holy, Lord God of hosts:
   Heaven and earth are full of thy glory:
   Glory be to thee, O Lord most high. Amen.

Most often we sing the first verse of the hymn:

Holy, holy, holy! Lord God Almighty!
Early in the morning our song shall rise to thee;
Holy, holy, holy! merciful and mighty;
God in three persons, blessed Trinity!

6. This period of prayer is lengthy, but from the prayer of the people through the eucharistic prayer there is participation by the people so that this does not become a long monologue by one pray-er.
7. This is usually followed by a participatory peace and benediction in which the people speak peace and blessing to one another.
8. *Companion to the Book of Services* (Nashville: Abingdon Press, 1988), p. 115.